RECORDS OF THE ROYAL MARINES

Royal Marine Subalterns. 2nd Lieutenant carrying Divisional Colours, by Eschauzier.

Reproduced by kind permission of the Director of the National Maritime Museum, London.

PRO READERS' GUIDE No 10

RECORDS OF THE ROYAL MARINES

by

Garth Thomas

PRO Publications

PRO Publications
Public Record Office
Chancery Lane, London
WC2A 1LR

ISBN 1 873162 19 7

A catalogue card for this book is available from the British Library

Printed by Multiplex Medway Ltd
Walderslade, Kent

FOREWORD

Who are these men holding Army rank and yet so obviously part of the naval forces? And why are they listed in all three of the *Navy List*, the *Army List* and the *Royal Marines List*? And why do they come in four divisions and two colours?

My purpose has been to provide the researcher with a guide to the wanted information about most aspects of the Royal Marines by the quickest route known to me. Some of the Royal Marines' records are gems of concision yet informativeness: the Records of Service provide a case in point. But the principles that underlay the selection of records for permanent preservation are sometimes no clearer to me than the principles of confusion that led to the dispersal of similar information throughout a number of record classes. I have made chapters and sections that seemed to me to have been prompted both by the nature of the documents thereunder discussed and also by the questions that members of the public have brought to me. The latter, in the majority of cases, to judge by the happy reception accorded to my guide to the records of the Militia, are less interested in archivists' analyses of the nature of such and such an archive than in receiving from specialist archivists the answer to the real question for which they are seeking the solutions, viz 'Has the information I want survived? If so, where can I find it?'

The conclusion has ineluctably borne in upon me, that it is impossible to write a coherent account of the Royal Marines based solely upon the official records that have been selected for permanent preservation. The records' survival rate has been haphazard in the extreme; and, given the general excellence of many of the surviving records, the losses are to be doubly deplored.

Public Record Office (PRO) references are supplied, prefixed with no specific identifying abbreviation, except in instances where papers and books or other publications — as distinct from original, unique records created by central government — referred to are known to be held, too, elsewhere: that is to indicate that other repositories or libraries will have their own means of reference. In cases where you are referred to documents held elsewhere, an easily recognizable abbreviation is prefixed to the repository's reference. In the case of records in classes such as WO 32, an indication of the code is provided to enable the researcher to locate and verify the reference in the class lists; it is not part of the document's reference and plays no part in placing an order for production of the file.

Researchers should be aware that, as a general rule, an official record is not available for public inspection for a period of thirty years, dating from the file's closure. In the case of personal records, the delay could well rise to seventy-five years. Yet again, some records are unavailable for periods of fifty or even 100 years; some are retained by the department of origin, in conformity with section 3(4) of the Public Records Act 1958 as amended. Information about opening dates is given in the class lists. The dates covered by each file are likewise stated in the class lists, so that it can easily be determined whether a wanted record is accessible or not.

For technical help in the production of this guide, it is a great pleasure for me, once again, to thank the team of Mr James Murray, Mr Melvyn Stainton, Miss Fiona Prothero, Mrs Julia Wigg and Dr Alfred Knightbridge, members of the Publications Department of the Public Record Office. My thanks go, too, to Mr Aidan Lawes and Dr Louise Atherton of the Reader Services Department at Chancery Lane, for help through the maze that is the State Papers. Mr Graham Stanley, of the Government Services Department, very kindly helped me to identify the most recent Royal Marines' records to have become available to the public.

Another source of great pleasure is to recall a very warm welcome at the Royal Marines Museum, Eastney, where staff gave valuable time to showing me around and answering my questions. No research focusing upon the Royal Marines is likely to be fully satisfactory without a visit to the museum and library.

London, May 1994. G.T.

GENERAL INFORMATION ABOUT THE PUBLIC RECORD OFFICE

At present the PRO is divided between two buildings. The records described in this **Reader's Guide** are housed at Kew. If you are in doubt about which to visit for other records, telephone 081-876-3444.

Public Record Office, Chancery Lane, London WC2A 1LR Tel: 081-876-3444
Opening hours: 9.30am to 5.00pm Monday to Friday; the Census Rooms are also open from 9.30am to 5.00pm on Saturdays. You do not need to make an appointment.
Closed on public holidays and for annual stocktaking (usually the first two weeks in October).
Museum and shop open 9.30am to 4.45pm.

Public Record Office, Ruskin Avenue, Kew, Surrey TW9 4DU Tel: 081-876-3444
Opening hours: 9.30 to 5.00pm Monday to Friday. You do not need to make an appointment.
Closed on public holidays and for annual stocktaking (usually the first two weeks in October).
Shop open 9.30am to 4.45pm.

In 1996 the Chancery Lane building will close and all records will be housed at Kew. Contact the NewPRO team on extension 2524 for details.

When you first visit the PRO, bring with you a formal document (eg: driving licence or cheque card) bearing your name and signature. If you are not a British citizen you will need to bring your passport or national identity card. You can then be issued, free of charge, with a Reader's Ticket. Without a Ticket you cannot be admitted to the Reading Rooms or order documents. You do not need one to visit the Census Room or the Museum at Chancery Lane.

You may only use pencils in the reading rooms. Pens of any kind are not allowed. You may use personal computers, typewriters and tape recorders in most of the reading rooms. For a full list of general and reading room rules, please ask for General Information Leaflet no 27: *Rules for Readers*.

Records in the PRO are divided into classes which reflect as far as possible their original administrative arrangement. Each class has its own lettercode identifying the government department or other body from which it originates: WO refers to War Office, T to Treasury and so on. Added to these letters is a class number which identifies records relating to a particular subject created by that department. The class ADM 157, for instance has the title of **Royal Marines Attestation Forms** and covers the years 1790-1912. Each class is then subdivided into smaller numbered items known as pieces or documents. ADM 157/1, for instance, refers to the attestation forms of the Chatham Division for 1790-1803 A-Z, and for 1804 A-O, (arranged alphabetically by surname). An example page from this document can be seen on p 44.

For details of records to be found in particular classes you should consult the class lists which can be seen in the PRO reference rooms.

TABLE SHOWING THE EVOLUTION OF THE ROYAL MARINES

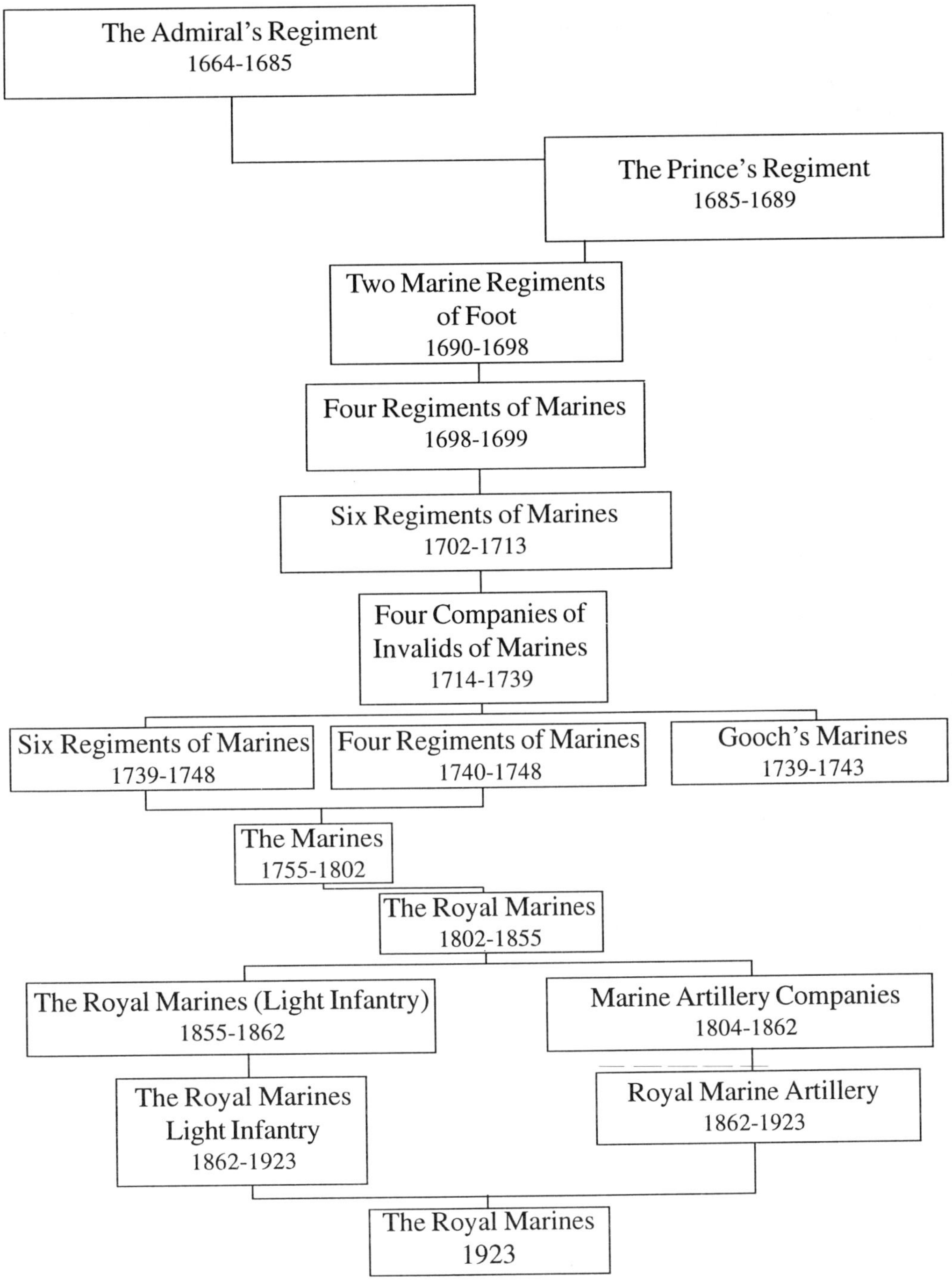

CONTENTS

1. Historical Introduction 1

2. General Records of the (Royal) Marines

2.1 Correspondence and Policy 4
2.2 (Royal) Marine Pay Office 4
2.3 Royal Marine Office (now Commandant General's Office 4
2.4 Rules and Instructions for the Better Governance of the Royal Marines 4
2.5 Unpublished Histories 5
2.6. Royal Marine Units Newspapers 5
2.7 Establishment 5
2.8 Quartering 6
2.9 Uniforms and Clothing 6

3. Divisional Records

3.1 Chatham Division 9
3.2 Deal Depot 11
3.3 Plymouth Division 12
3.4 Portsmouth Division 14
3.5 Royal Marine Artillery 16
3.6 Woolwich Division 17
3.7 Miscellaneous Records 18
3.8 Royal Marine Units Serving Overseas 19
3.9 Letter Books and Order Books covering all Divisions 20
3.10 Correspondence between the Royal Marine Office and Admiralty 21

4. Pay and Accounts

4.1 Pay 22
4.1.1 General 22
4.1.2 Arrears from1748 22
4.1.3 Paymasters 23
4.1.4 Paymasters' Agents 23

4.1.5 Half Pay and Allowances 23
4.1.6 Retired Pay 24
4.1.7 Recruiting 24
4.1.8 Parity with Other Services 24
4.1.9 Personal Financial Prospects 24
4.1.10 Savings Bank 24
4.1.11 Pay and Service Conditions of Officers, 1883 24
4.1.12 Twentieth-Century Pay Records 25
4.2 Accounts 25

5. Military Operations and Reorganization in the Twentieth Century
5.1 Introduction 26
5.2 War Diaries 26
5.2.1 First World War 26
5.2.2 Second World War 27
5.2.3 Korean War 29
5.2.4 The Falklands War and the Persian Gulf War 29
5.3. Miscellaneous Papers of the Second World War Period 30
5.3.1 Second World War Establishment Records 30
5.3.2 Royal Marines Commandos 30
5.3.3 Royal Marines Boom Patrol Detachment 30
5.4. Post War Organization and Training 30
5.4.1 Ministry of Defence Records 30
5.4.2 Cabinet Office Records 31
5.4.3 Defence Council Records 32
5.5 Amphibious Warfare: Miscellaneous Units 32
5.5.1 Amphibian Support Regiment, Royal Marines 32
5.5.2 Amphibious School, Royal Marines 32
5.5.3 Amphibious Warfare Experimental Establishment (AWEE) 33
5.5.4 Royal Marines Signal School 33
5.5.5 Special Boat Section, Royal Marines (SBS, RM) 33
5.5.6 N° 3 (Royal Marines) Commando 33
5.5.7 N° 41 (Royal Marines) Commando 33
5.5.8 N° 46 (Royal Marines) Commando 33
5.6 Co-operation between Royal Marines and United States Marine Corps 33

6. Ceremonies and War Memorials
6.1 Ceremonies 34
6.2 War Memorials 34

7. Medical, Educational and Musical Records
7.1 Hospital Records 35
7.1.1 Hospital Records of the Eighteenth and Nineteenth Centuries 35
7.1.2 Hospital Records of the First World War 35
7.1.3 Hospital Records of the Second World War 35
7.1.4 Medical and Hospital Records of the Post Second World War Period 35
7.2 Royal Marines School and Teachers 36
7.3 Royal Marines Bands and Music 36

8. Service Records
8.1 Officers 37
8.1.1 Publications 37
8.1.2 Official Records Prior to 1793 37
8.1.3 Official Records Post 1793 39
8.1.4 Individual Cases 40
8.2 Warrant Officers 40
8.3 Royal Marine Chaplains 40
8.3.1 Second Regiment Chaplains 41
8.3.2 Chaplains who formerly were Marines 41
8.4 Royal Marine Surgeons 41
8.4.1 First Regiment 41
8.4.2 Second Regiment 42
8.5 Other Ranks 42
8.5.1 Introduction 42
8.5.2 Attestations (ADM 157) 43
8.5.3 Description Books (ADM 158) 45
8.5.4 Records of Service (ADM 159) 45
8.5.5 Effective and Subsistence Lists (ADM 96) 46
8.5.6 HM Ships' Muster Rolls and Crew Lists (ADM 36 and ADM 37) 47
8.5.7 Lady Marines 47

9. Other Service Records

9.1 Medals 48
9.2 Courts Martial 48
9.3 Obituary Books and Casualty Records 50
9.4 Hospital Records 51
9.5 Prisoners of War 51
9.6 Coastguard Service of Royal Marines 51
9.7 Royal Marine Census 1922 51
9.8 Mobilization Returns and Complements of HM Ships 51
9.9 Ecclesiastical, Civil and Census Records 52
9.10 Desertion 52
9.11 Pension Records of Royal Marines 53
9.12 Pensions awarded to Royal Marines' Families 53
9.13 Wills and Administrations 53

10. Records of Royal Marines' Families

10.1 Next-of-Kin 54
10.2 Registers of Births, Marriages and Deaths 54
10.3 Widows and Children: Pensions, Wills and Administrations 54
10.4 Orphans of Royal Marines 54

Appendixes

1 Pull-out table showing the distribution of Companies throughout the Divisions *following page* 54
2 Hints on identifying a Royal Marines' Division 55
3 Some addresses of other record repositories 56

Bibliography 61

Index 62

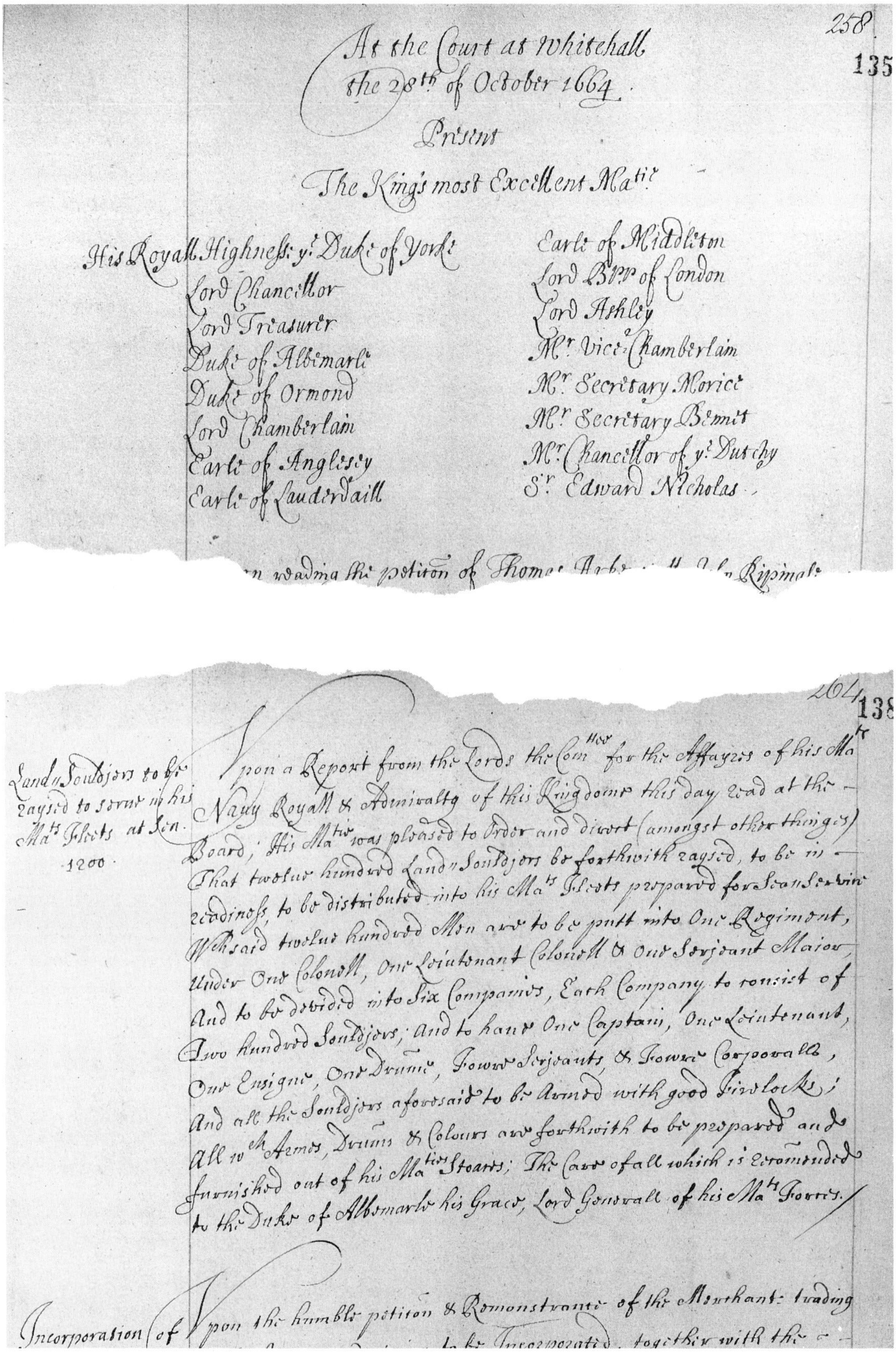

258
135

At the Court at Whitehall
the 28th of October 1664.
Present
The King's most Excellent Matie

His Royall Highness ye Duke of Yorke
Lord Chancellor
Lord Treasurer
Duke of Albemarle
Duke of Ormond
Lord Chamberlain
Earle of Anglesey
Earle of Lauderdaill

Earle of Middleton
Lord Bpp of London
Lord Ashley
Mr Vice Chamberlain
Mr Secretary Morice
Mr Secretary Bennett
Mr Chancellor of ye Dutchy
Sr Edward Nicholas.

264
138

Land Souldjers to be raysed to serve in his Mats Fleets at Sea. 1200

Upon a Report from the Lords the Comrs for the Affayres of his Maty Navy Royall & Admiralty of this Kingdome this day read at the Board; His Matie was pleased to Order and direct (amongst other things) That twelve hundred Land Souldjers be forthwith raysed, to be in readiness, to be distributed into his Mats Fleets prepared for Sea Service Which said twelve hundred Men are to be putt into One Regiment, Under One Colonell, One Leiutenant Colonell & One Serjeant Maior, And to be devided into Six Companies, Each Company to consist of Two hundred Souldjers; And to have One Captain, One Leiutenant, One Ensigne, One Drume, Fower Serjeants & Fower Corporalls, And all the Souldjers aforesaid to be Armed with good Firelocks; And all wch Armes, Drums & Colours are forthwith to be prepared and furnished out of his Maties Stoares; The Care of all which is recomended to the Duke of Albemarle his Grace, Lord Generall of his Mats Forces.

Incorporation of

Upon the humble petition & Remonstrance of the Merchant trading

Figure 1. PC 2/57. *Above*: the names of those attending the meeting of the Privy Council held on 28 October 1664 (f 258). *Below*: the Order in Council authorizing the raising of 1200 land soldiers 'to be distributed into His Majesty's Fleets' (f 264).

1. HISTORICAL INTRODUCTION

By an Order in Council of 28 October 1664, Charles II authorized the raising of a regiment of 1,200 Land Soldiers to be known as the Duke of York and Albany's Maritime Regiment of Foot (and because His Royal Highness was Lord High Admiral, it came also to be known as the Admiral's Regiment, to distinguish it from the General's Regiment) 'to be distributed into His Majesty's Fleets prepared for Sea Service' (Privy Council Office Register, C II, vol 4, f 264 [PC 2/57, f 264]) **[Fig 1]** His reasons can only be surmised, but may well have been to obviate the inconvenience caused by Army reductions and to maintain naval discipline. As Britain's naval role evolved, the need for well trained 'sea soldiers' became apparent, for the land army conspicuously lacked shipboard experience and skills[1].

For some considerable time thereafter, notwithstanding, soldiers continued to be drawn off from regiments and garrison companies of the regular army for sea service, as the need arose. Records of soldiers so supplied appear in State Papers Domestic, Charles II, Declared Accounts (Army) and Declared Accounts (Navy) of the Audit Office (record class AO 1) and the Privy Council Office registers; others lie scattered throughout the Miscellaneous Records of the War Office (WO 26). When, in 1685, the Duke of York came to the throne as King James II, the Admiral's Regiment passed to his son-in-law, the hereditary Prince of Denmark, Prince George. In 1690 Prince George of Denmark's Maritime Regiment of Foot was disbanded and replaced by two regiments exclusively designated for sea service. The first Commissions were dated 16 and 17 January 1690 (SP 44/166, f 82) and followed by Beating Orders for recruitment (SP 44/166, ff 81, 84 and 85). Towards the end of that same year, a statement of the organization of the two regiments was drawn up (State Papers, Domestic, King William's Chest [SP 8/8]). Parliament authorized the raising of Six Marine Regiments in 1702. The raising commenced between 14 and 16 March 1701/2, when the colonels were named and the place of rendezvous appointed (WO 26/11, pp 34-36). On 26 March 1701/2 statistics relative to the establishment were produced (WO 26/11, pp 40-41). The Royal Warrant for the mustering of the six new Regiments was signed by Queen Anne on 9 April 1702 (WO 26/11, p 45). The Out-Letters of the Secretary at War take up the story in 1705. On 3 April 1705 the composition of the companies in the regiments of the English and of the Irish establishments were fixed (WO 4/3, page 201). On 12 April 1705 the names of the colonels were again given and the establishments of the Six Regiments repeated. The pay voucher for the additional 5,000 men raised was prepared for the Treasury on 21 May 1705 (WO 4/3, p 252).

On 16 May 1702 a **Marine Pay Office** was established as a separate entity. Nevertheless, the size, number and indeed the very existence of the Marine regiments continued to fluctuate in rhythm with the exigencies of war. At the Peace of Utrecht in 1713 a general reduction of the Army took place, and the Six Marine Regiments were disbanded (SP

[1] Only major stages in the evolution of the Marines will be mentioned here. Historians will undertake closer study of the Privy Council records, State Papers Domestic of each reign, State Papers Domestic (later Home Office) Military Entry Books, War Office records, Admiralty records, Treasury records and the *London Gazette* in particular among public records in order to draw up a more detailed account.

44/172, p 282). A more or less notional list of regiments for sea service, invalids in effect, was maintained thereafter, until Parliament decided upon re-establishing Marine regiments in 1739[2]. But once again, in 1748, the Marines were disbanded. It is the Treasury records that tell the story of the financial hardship that disbandment entailed for the Marines.

Marines

We have much pleasure in announcing the following distinguished mark of His Majesty's most gracious approbation of the services of that highly-gallant and useful corps, the Marines.

Admiralty Office, 29th April.

'The Earl St Vincent having signified to my Lords Commissioners of the Admiralty that His Majesty, in order to mark his Royal approbation of the very meritorious conduct of the Corps of Marines during the late war, has been graciously pleased to direct that the Corps shall in future be styled the *Royal Marines.*

'I have great satisfaction in obeying their Lordships commands to communicate this intelligence to you, and in offering their Lordships congratulations on this testimony of the opinion His Majesty entertains of the very distinguished services of that part of his forces to which you belong. I am, &c.

(signed) 'EVAN NEPEAN'

To Lt-Gen. SOUTER JOHNSTONE,
Commander of the Marines

A copy of the above letter was read to the Marines on their parade, and received with enthusiastic gratitude.

In consequence of this honourable distinction, the facings of their uniform are altered from white to blue.

The Peace-Establishment of the Royal Marines is to be 100 companies of 100 men each: 30 are to belong to the division at Chatham, 35 to that of Portsmouth, and 35 to the Plymouth-division.

Figure 2 Copy of an extract from Steel's *List of the Royal Navy,*June 1802, p 43, announcing the style ***ROYAL*** Marines, 29 April 1802.

[2] Full references are provided by A J Marini, 'Parliament and the Marine Regiments, 1739', *The Mariner's Mirror* 62, 1976, pp 55-65. Marini presents a case for seeing, in the government thinking of the time, a foretaste of the decision taken in 1755 to establish the Marines on a permanent basis as sea soldiers, no longer *ad hoc* units embarked in emergencies.

Control of those early Marines was committed to military and naval authority respectively, according to whether the Marines were on shore or at sea. The clash of what would later be called 'powers of command', nevertheless, created some unfortunate episodes.

On 3 April 1755 another Order in Council approved the raising of 5,000 Marines, who were grouped into fifty companies, each of which was assigned to one or other of three 'Grand Divisions', quartered respectively at Chatham, Plymouth and Portsmouth, under the control of the Board of Admiralty. Thus was established that distinctive feature of the Marines, that can be summed up in the phrase: 'The Marines have a home'. They belong to their Division, which, unlike the Army in its early days, provided the Marines with barrack accommodation. It was an exceptional case for a Marine to move to another Division. The number of Companies steadily grew; and the Marines were never again disbanded.

The Marines were designated 'Royal' by King George III in an order dated 29 April 1802, on the recommendation of Lord St Vincent[1] **[Fig 2]**.

From 1805 to 1869 there was a further Division, quartered at Woolwich. On the disbandment of the Woolwich Division, the Royal Marines were distributed among the other Divisions; but, according to what principle, is no longer known. In 1848 the Portsmouth Division moved to Forton Barracks, Gosport; and in 1861 a Depot was established at Walmer, Kent, which later became the Royal Marine Depot, Deal. The 'Companies' within each Division were purely administrative units, that bore no relation to the 'Tactical Companies' of Battalions formed when the Marines were on active service. Tactical Companies might contain men drawn from several Divisional Companies.

Up until 1804, artillery services to the Royal Navy had been provided, as and when required, by the Royal Artillery. In 1804, however, that arrangement ceased: and an Order in Council authorized the creation of Marine Companies of Artillery to be attached to the Divisions. The number of those Artillery Companies varied in accordance with the prevailing military situation: during the comparatively peaceful interlude of the 1830s, for example, there were only two, both attached to the Portsmouth Division. In 1859 the Royal Marine Artillery was formed as a distinct Division, for which Eastney Barracks were built. The historical record, covering the period August 1804 to February 1873, is in ADM 201/31.

In 1855 the infantry section of the Royal Marines took the name Royal Marine Light Infantry.

A major reorganization of the Royal Marines took place in 1869, in which the Woolwich Division was distributed among the other Divisions. The records, October 1869 to March 1881, are in ADM 201/29 and 30. Records of the Royal Marine Reserve, October 1899 to December 1904, are in ADM 201/33. In 1929 the Royal Marine Light Infantry (RMLI)('Red Marines') and the Royal Marine Artillery (RMA)('Blue Marines') merged to form the single Royal Marine Corps. The subsequent events in the life of the Royal Marines will be found in the section concerning post-war reorganization.

I am far from having exhausted the archival resources; and the academic, critical history of the Royal Marines still awaits its author. But enough has already been set down to indicate the main, organizational and administrative evolution of the Marines in which the official records took shape.

---

[1] See Lord St Vincent's Memoirs for his reflections on the marines.

2. GENERAL RECORDS OF THE (ROYAL) MARINES

2.1 Correspondence and Policy

Correspondence and papers on policy matters, including the raising and deployment of Marine Companies, are to be found in several classes of records. The In-Letters of the Admiralty include a special section of letters from Marine (from 1802, Royal Marine) officers, 1787 to 1839 (ADM 1/3246-3357). Other documents concerning Marines and placed in the same record class of Admiralty In-Letters (ADM 1), can be identified and located by using the Indexes and Digests that constitute record class ADM 12. The Out-Letters of the Admiralty, too, include a special section of letters to and concerning Marines, 1703 to 1845 (ADM 2/1147-1251).

2.2 (Royal) Marine Pay Office

The records of the (Royal) Marine Pay Office (ADM 96) include In- and Out-Letter Books, ledgers and accounts, effective and subsistence lists. The Royal Marine Pay Office was absorbed into the Office of the Accountant General of the Navy in 1831, which, in turn, was subsumed under the Paymaster General's Department in 1835. The classes which contain those records will be discussed further.

2.3 Royal Marine Office, now Commandant General's Office

The records of the Royal Marine Office include a series of general letter books, for correspondence with all Divisions, for the years 1803 to 1868 (ADM 56); thereafter, there are separate series of letter books for the affairs of each Division (ADM 57 to ADM 63), and for correspondence with the Admiralty (ADM 191) and with the War Office (ADM 200). General correspondence and papers of the Royal Marine Office, which include historical compilations and statistical returns — are to be found in ADM 201.

2.4 Rules and Instructions for the Better Governance of the Royal Marines

The Rules and Instructions as promulgated by Queen Anne, 1 July 1702, are in WO 26/11, ff 276- 281 (= pages 191 to 195 of older references). They deal with such matters as the quartering of Marines near major naval ports, the pay and provisions of Marines and their mustering. The latter posed a very great difficulty, as the War Office's method of mustering was regiment based, whereas only comparatively small groups of Marines went aboard each ship, with the result that a long period of time could elapse before a regiment could be mustered in its entirety and paid.

The revised Rules and Instructions of 1740 are in WO 26/19.

Sea Instructions and Shore Instructions, 1759, are in ADM 96/3.

A search through the Acts of Parliament will furnish you with numerous laws laying down Regulations and Instructions for the Royal Marines, which cover not only matters of behaviour, but also the forms and returns to be filled in by each unit. Each volume is indexed. The PRO Library holds a complete run, though divided between the Kew and Chancery Lane sites. Readers should request the volumes wanted from the staff in the Reference Room at Kew. The British Library and the House of Lords Record Office both hold full sets, as do most research libraries. Some off-prints are likewise held by the PRO library, viz the *Rules and Articles for the Better Government of His Majesty's Royal Marine Forces while on Shore*, before 1805, and the *Rules and Articles for the Better Government of His Majesty's Royal Marine Forces, Established the 15th August 1805*, bound together to form one volume (PRO library reference MN.180.007). The *Rules and Articles Established by the Commissions For executing the Office of Lord High Admiral of the United Kingdom of Great Britain and Ireland and The Better Government Of His Majesty's Royal Marine Forces While on Shore, From the 24th of March 1809*, London: George Eyre and Andrew Strahan, 1809, is held by the PRO library under reference MN.180.007. And so, too, is a copy of *An Act for the Regulation of His Majesty's Royal Marine Forces, while on Shore,* London: Eyre and Strahan, 1809[1].

Among the records of the Royal Marine Office is a Note Book containing an alphabetical index of instructions and regulations affecting the Royal Marines, 1884 to 1898 (ADM 201/14), together with a second Note Book, containing similar material for the years 1883 to 1900 (ADM 201/15). General Standing Orders for the years 1893, 1902, 1910 and 1922 have survived and are in ADM 64.

2.5 Unpublished Histories

A number of manuscript histories of the Royal Marines, or at least of sections of the corps, have been preserved. Historical notes and extracts relating to Royal Marines, originally held at HM Dockyard, Chatham, and covering the years 1761 to 1827, are in ADM 201/50. There are two reports on the work of the Corps of Royal Marines: one covers the years 1907 to 1909 (ADM 201/58), the other is for the year 1922 (ADM 201/66). A History of the Royal Marines Engineers, 1939 to 1946, is in ADM 201/106. Finally, a History of N° 46 (Royal Marine) Commando, 1942 to 1945, is to be found in DEFE 2/977, and the history of the Royal Marines Boom Patrol Detachment, 1942 to 1948, in DEFE 2/988.

2.6 Royal Marine Units Newspapers

Royal Marine unit newspapers were issued on a monthly basis by the Officer Commanding Royal Marine Commando units, 1960 to 1978 (ADM 301). They contain information about operations, recreation and photographs. The units for which such newspapers survive are as follows: N° 40 (RM) Commando (ADM 301/1 to 6); N° 41 (RM) Commando (ADM 301/12-18); N° 42 (RM) Commando (ADM 301/19-20); N° 43 (RM) Commando (ADM 301/21-29); 3 Commando Brigade, Royal Marines, 1950 and 1951 (ADM 301/30)[2]; 3 Commando Brigade, Air Squadron, 1974 and 1965 (ADM 301/31 and 32); 3 Commando Brigade, Headquarters Signals, 1972-1978 (ADM 301/33); and the Commando Logistics Regiments, 1973-1978 (ADM 301/34).

2.7 Establishment

Copies of establishment returns and statements of conditions of service of the Marine Regiments, 1690 to 1708, are in ADM 7/832.

In addition to the official sources of information concerning the annual establishment and estimates vote, manuscript notes added to the *Marines Lists* in record class ADM 118, and which appear authentic, should provide a convenient means of obtaining establishment figures of the years for which the annotations were made.

---

[1] 49 Geo III, cap xix, dated 24 March 1809.

[2] Retained by the Ministry of Defence, under section 3(4) of the Public Records Act 1958, as amended.

For purposes of planning forces to send against the Boers, a return, showing numbers of all ranks of Royal Marines available for mobilization, was prepared in 1898 (ADM 201/52). That return was followed by another, showing the numbers of Royal Marines entered, discharged and deserted, November 1899 to January 1900 (ADM 201/53).

Between 1903 and 1924 the Royal Marine Office prepared a series of 'Statistical Packets', providing statistical returns of Royal Marine personnel in various categories (ADM 201/54-69). Earlier statistical papers included the pressed copies of Returns to the Admiralty, February 1869 to July 1881 (ADM 201/70), and an incomplete return of officers, warrant and non-commissioned officers and men, ashore and afloat, July 1884 to May 1898 (ADM 201/71).

2.8 Quartering

Records concerning the quartering arrangements of 1689 have been identified as follows. Those dated 8 February 1690 are in SP 44/166, f 88. Those for the end of March 1690 are in SP 44/166, f 93. A wider search through the State Papers, Domestic, Military Entry Books (in record class SP 44, held at Chancery Lane), should lead easily to the identification of others, as the volumes are indexed, either at the end, or continuously in the margin against the entry. There is a general index to Military and Treasury Books, 1679 to 1783, in IND 8914 (held at Chancery Lane).

2.9 Uniforms and Clothing

The distinctive yellow coats with red linings and red stockings of the first Marines are said have been in accordance with the personal taste of the Duke of York. Reference to that original colour scheme persisted in subsequent modifications of the uniform and is still to be found in the dress of the Royal Marine of today. Early descriptions of the Marines' dress are indirect, in that they are derived from the descriptions of deserters, such as those given in the *London Gazette* of 5 to 8 January 1684/5, and 9 to 13 April 1684 (ZJ 1/11). On taking command of the Marine Regiments, Prince George of Denmark, whose tastes ran to 'fancy waistcoats', changed the colour scheme. Subsequent commanders did similarly. As far as I have been able to determine, the information concerning those changes is not to be found in official records, but rather in private papers, letters and the like, which are not in the custody of the PRO. The standard histories of the Royal Marines are still the best guide for you in this area.

Nevertheless, you may be able to glean some information about a Marine's dress from the Divisional Orders, such as those for Chatham Division, dated 4 March 1757. The *London Gazette* of 5 to 9 May 1747, when it was proposed to place the Marines entirely under Admiralty control, published an Order for the 'Clothing of H.M. Ten Regiments of Marines' (ZJ 1/43). However, as the Marines were disbanded the year following, it is unlikely that the order was ever carried into effect. Records concerning the early eighteenth-century sea kit of Marines when embarked are contained in a document entitled 'A Scheme for Maintaining a Body of Marine-Forces', [1725], in WO 55/1819.

A valuable source of information for the evolution of the uniforms of the Marines, and other branches of the Armed Forces, was published in only fifty copies in 1743, and entitled *Description of the Clothing of His Majesty's Bands of Gentlemen Pensioners, Yeomen of the Guard and Regiments of Footguards, Foot, Marines and Invalids on the Establishments of Great Britain and Ireland.* A copy is held by the British Library and by the Bodleian Library, Oxford, and a reprint is held by the Victoria and Albert Museum, South Kensington. A copy was also in the War Office Library, and a defective copy in the Royal Artillery Officers' library at Woolwich. To my knowledge, neither has been placed in the custody of the PRO.

A single file containing clothing production accounts, 1877 to 1897, is to be found in ADM 201/13.

Records concerning the new design of the Royal Crown and Cypher, 1952 to 1954, are in ADM 201/104.

Dress Regulations for Royal Marine officers appeared in the annual *Navy Lists* from the latter half of the nineteenth to the early years of the twentieth centuries. The *Navy Lists* are on open access shelves in the Reference Room, and are held, too, by major research libraries.

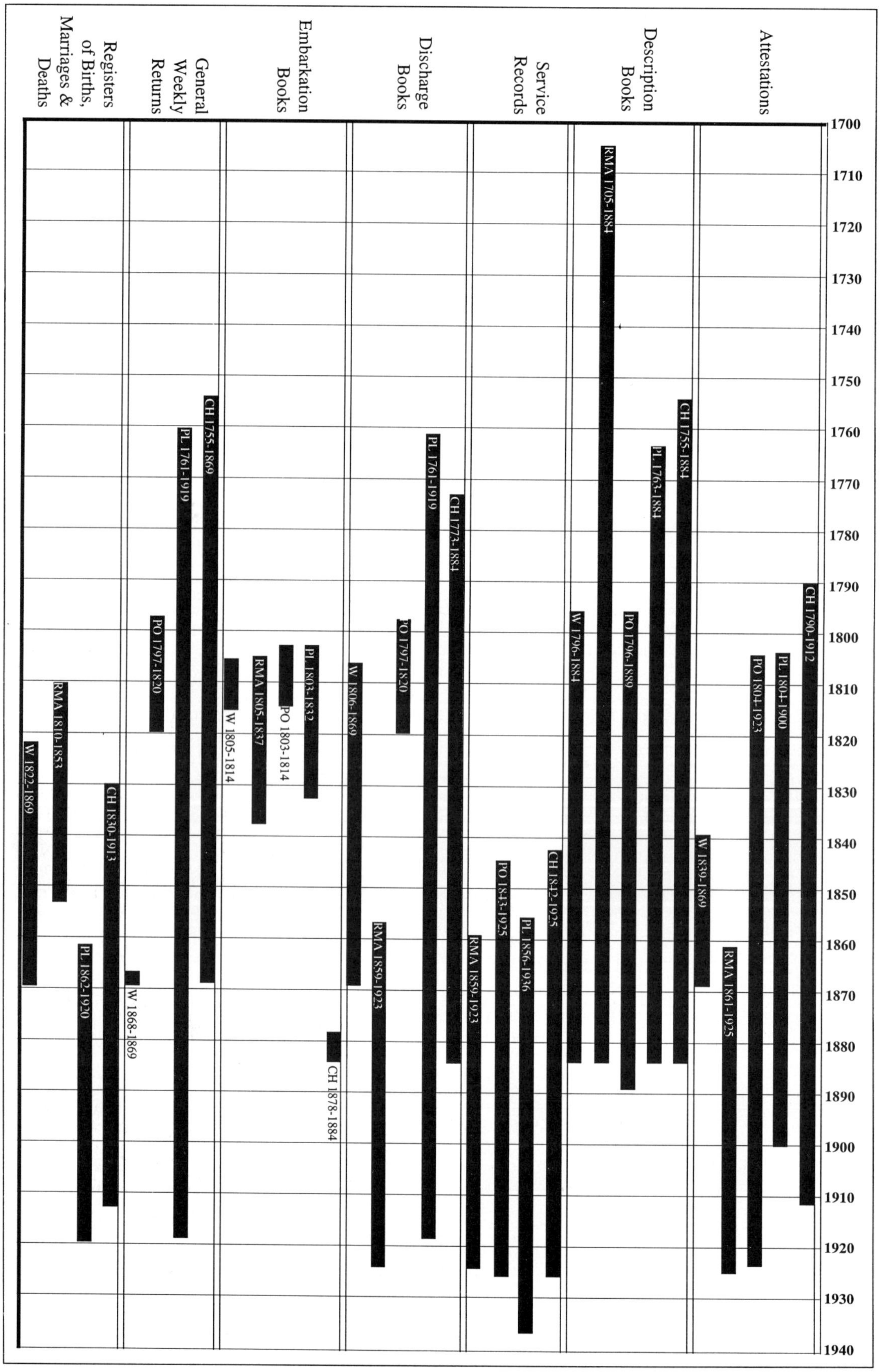

Figure 3. Distribution of some major records

3. DIVISIONAL RECORDS

Each Divisional Headquarters maintained its own records; there are very few instances of records covering all Divisions. It follows, then, that for information about a Royal Marine or his Company or his Division, it is advisable to know the Division prior to embarking upon the search. A complicating factor for research is the very uneven survival rate of Royal Marines' records, as the following table concerning personal records will illustrate.

	CH	PL	PO	RMA	W
Attestations	1790-1912	1804-1900	1804-1923	1861-1925	1839-1869
Description Books	1755-1884	1763-1884	1796-1889	1705-1884	1796-1884
Service Records	1842-1925	1856-1936	1843-1925	1859-1923	-
Discharge Books	1773-1884	1761-1919	1797-1820	1859-1923	1806-1869
Embarkation Books	1878-1884	1803-1832	1803-1814	1805-1837	1805-1814
General Weekly Returns	1755-1869	1761-1919	1797-1820	-	1868-1869
Registers of births, marriages and deaths	1830-1913	1862-1920	-	1810-1853	1822-1869

The lists that follow gather together the Divisional records, showing dates for which each category has survived, and indicating the PRO references.

3.1 CHATHAM DIVISION

Records of Individuals

Attestations, 1790-1883 (by date of enlistment)	ADM 157/1-139
Attestations, 1842-1912	ADM157/1276-1851
Indexes to Attestations for which no Register has survived, 1914-1918	ADM 313/1

Description Books, 1755-1884	ADM 158/1-32
Registers of Service, 1842-1935	ADM 159/36-60, 124-142
Indexes to Registers, 1842-1925	ADM 313/55-79
Register of RMLI Short Service, 1914-1918	ADM 159/143-149
Index to Register of RMLI Short Service, 1914-1918	ADM 313/84
General Weekly Returns, 1755-1869	ADM 183/42-98
Embarkation Books, 1878-1884	ADM 183/99
Muster Rolls of HM Ships, 1883	ADM 183/100
Discharge Books, 1773-1884	ADM 183/101-110
Disposal Books, 1814-1886	ADM 183/111-113
Registers of Marriages, 1864-1884	ADM 183/114-115
Registers of Marriages and of Births of Children, 1830-1884	ADM 183/116-117
Registers of Marriages and of Births and Deaths of Children, 1862-1913	ADM 183/118-119

Unpublished History

Historical notes and extracts relating to the Royal Marines at Chatham, 1761-1827	ADM 201/50

Order Books

Order Books, 1867-1941	ADM 183/1-37

Courts Martial Records

Registers, 1902-1905	ADM 194/1
Royal Marine China Battalion: **Chatham**, Woolwich and 1st Battalion ranks, 1857-1860 (Overseas)	ADM 194/39

Royal Navy Officers and Ratings, 1803-1856	ADM 13/103-104
Royal Navy Officers and Ratings, and Royal Marines, 1812-1915	ADM 194/42
Royal Navy Officers, 1857-1915	ADM 194/43-45
Royal Navy and Royal Marines, 1911 onwards	ADM 156

Divisional Letter Books

Adjutant-General RM's Letter Book to Chatham, 1869-1884	ADM 58/1-21
Admiralty Letters: to Chatham, 1755-1826	ADM 183/121-125
Letter Books: from Chatham, 1823-1884	ADM 183/126-129

3.2 DEAL DEPOT

Records of Individuals

Registers of Service, 1866-1925	ADM 159/113-118
Description Books, 1881-1940	ADM 158/284-299
Disposal Book, 1874-188	ADM 193/1-2
Attestations, RM Labour Corps, Short Service, 1914-1918 (numerical arrangement)	ADM 157/3270-3458
Index to RM Labour Corps, Short Service, 1914-1919	ADM 313/2
Registers to RM Labour Corps, 1917-1919	ADM 159/122-123
Attestations, RM Engineers, (numerical arrangement)	ADM 157/3467-3625
Registers of Service, RM Divisional Engineers, 1914-1916	ADM 159/119-121

Courts Martial Records

Royal Navy Officers and Ratings 1803-1856	ADM 13/103-104
Royal Navy Officers and Ratings and Royal Marines, 1812-1855	ADM 194/42
Royal Navy Officers, 1857-1915	ADM 194/43-45
Royal Navy and Royal Marines, 1911 onwards	ADM 156

Letter Books

Adjutant-General RM's Letter Book: to Deal, 1868-1884	ADM 62/1-18

See also **Miscellaneous Records**

3.3 PLYMOUTH DIVISION

Records of Individuals

Attestations, 1804-1838 (by date of enlistment)	ADM 157/140
Attestations and Discharges, 1842-1883	ADM 157/141-337
Attestations and Discharges, 1884-1900	ADM157/1852-1868
Description Books, 1763-1894	ADM 158/207-283
Registers of Service, 1856-1903	ADM 159/61-79
Indexes to Registers of Service, 1856-1903	ADM 313/80-81
Registers of Service of RMLI, 1902-1936	ADM 159/150-174
Registers of RMLI Short Service, 1914-1918	ADM 159/175-180
Registers of RMLI Short Service, 1914-1918	ADM 159/175-180

Index to Registers of RMLI Short Service, 1914-1918	ADM 313/109
General Weekly Returns, 1761-1919	ADM 184/24-34
Embarkation Books, 1803-1809 and 1819-1832	ADM 184/36-37
Discharge Books, 1784-1892	ADM 184/38-41
Disposal Books, 1788-1897	ADM 184/42
Registers of Marriages, and of Births and Deaths of Children, 1862-1920	ADM 184/43-54

Order Books

Order Books, 1760-1881	ADM 184/1-14
Commanding Officers' Order Books, 1833-1836	ADM 184/15-16
Pembroke Dock Divisional Order Books, 1845-1850	ADM 184/17-18
Garrison Order Book, 1873	ADM 184/19

Courts Martial Records

Registers, 1845-1898	ADM 194/21-32
District Courts Martial Registers, 1898-1902	ADM 194/33
District and Regimental Courts Martial Registers, 1902-1914	ADM 194/34-38
Registers: North Coast of Spain Battalion (Plymouth Division), 1836-1834	ADM 194/20
Royal Navy Officers and Ratings, 1803-1856	ADM 13/103-104
Royal Navy Officers and Ratings, and Royal Marines, 1812-1855	ADM 194/42

Royal Navy Officers, 1857-1915	ADM 194/43-45
Royal Navy and Royal Marines, 1911 onwards	ADM 156

Letter Books

Adjutant-General RM's Letter Books: to Plymouth, 1868-1884	ADM 60/1-17

3.4 PORTSMOUTH DIVISION

Records of Individuals

Attestations, 1804-1836 (by date of enlistment)	ADM 157/338-352
Index to Attestations, RM Ranks removed to RMA, 1834-1835	ADM313/3 (Index to ADM 157/664)
Attestations and Discharges, 1837-1883	ADM 157/353-615
Attestations and Discharges, 1869-1904	ADM 157/1869-2057
Attestations and Discharges, 1904-1923	ADM 157/2471-2847
Description Books, 1796-1888	ADM 158/91-206
Registers of Service, 1842-1901	ADM 159/1-19
Registers of RMLI Service, 1901-1925	ADM 159/181-202
Index to RMLI Service, 1901-1925	ADM 313/27-51
Registers of RMLI Short Service, 1914-1918	ADM 159/203-208
Index to RMLI Short Service, 1914-1918	ADM 313 (None available)
General Weekly Returns, 1797-1814	ADM 185/38-61
Embarkation Books, 1803-1814	ADM 185/62

Discharge Books, 1816-1888	ADM 185/63-67
Disposal Books, 1874-1881	ADM 185/68
Register of Marriages, 1869-1881	ADM 185/69
Garrison and Divisional Books, 1809-1941	ADM 185/1-33
Courts Martial Records	
Registers, 1834-1916	ADM 194/2-17
Registers: Royal Marine Detachment (Portsmouth Division) in HM Ships, 1836-1839 and 1859-1874	ADM 194/18-19
Royal Navy Officers and Ratings, 1803-1856	ADM 13/103-104
Royal Navy Officers and Ratings, and Royal Marines, 1812-1855	ADM 194/42
Royal Navy Officers, 1857-1915	ADM 194/43-45
Royal Navy and Royal Marines, 1911 onwards	ADM 156
Letter Books	
Adjutant-General RM's Letter Books: to Portsmouth, 1868-1884	ADM 60/1-17
Letter Books: from Portsmouth, 1772-1853	ADM 185/71-79
Miscellaneous Letters: from Portsmouth 1816-1922 and 1899-1906	ADM 185/82-81
Letter Books: to Admiralty, 1789-1817	ADM 185/82-104
Letters from the RM Barracks at Portsmouth and Gosport to the RM Office, 1833-1870	ADM 201/2

3.5 ROYAL MARINE ARTILLERY

Records of Individuals

Attestations, 1861-1918 (nominal order)	ADM 157/2848-2849
Attestations, 1869-1923	ADM 157/2850-3246
Certificates of Service, 1899-1925	ADM 157/3247- 3269
Description Books, 1705-1884	ADM 158/75, 77-90,101, 108, 114, 119, 124, 129, 137, 155, 161, 167, 171, 176, 182, 188, 194, 200, 205
Registers of Service, 1859-1923	ADM 159/20-35, 80-94
Indexes to Registers of Service, 1859-1923	ADM 313/52-54
Registers of Short Service, 1914-1920	ADM 159/95-102
Index to Registers of Short Service, 1914-1920	ADM 313/82
Embarkation Books, 1805-1837	ADM 193/7
Disposal Books, 1845-1859	ADM 159/8
Register of Marriages and Baptisms, 1810-1853	ADM 193/9

Order Books

Order Books, 1890-1918	ADM 193/3-6

Orderly Book

Daily Notes and Orders of Officer Commanding RMA Brigade Depot, 1917-1918	ADM 193/10

Courts Martial Records

Royal Navy Officers and Ratings, 1803-1856	ADM 13/103-104
Royal Navy Officers and Ratings, and Royal Marines, 1812-1855	ADM 194/42

Royal Navy Officers, 1957-1915	ADM 194/43-45
Royal Navy and Royal Marines, 1911 onwards	ADM 156

Letter Books

Adjutant-General RM's Letter Books: to Royal Marines Artillery, 1868-1884	ADM 59/1-17
RM Office: Correspondence and papers relating to the Royal Marine Artillery, 1804-1873	ADM 201/31

See also **Miscellaneous Records**

3.6 WOOLWICH DIVISION

Records of Individuals

Attestations and Discharges, 1839-1869	ADM 157/665-1275
Lists of Personnel of the Divisions, 1806-1822	ADM 6/407
Description Books, 1805-1884	ADM 158/33-90
General Weekly Returns, 1806-1822	ADM 81/10
Embarkation Books, 1805-1869	ADM 81/11
Discharge Books, 1806-1869	ADM 81/12-22
Marriage Roll, 1822-1853	ADM 81/23
Register of Marriages, 1852-1869	ADM 81/24
Register of Children's Baptisms, 1824-1868	ADM 81/25

Order Books

None surviving

Courts Martial Records

Royal Marine China Battalion: Chatham, **Woolwich** and 1st Battalion ranks, 1857-1860 (Overseas)	ADM 194/39

Woolwich and 2nd Battalion ranks, 1857-1860 (Overseas)	ADM 194/40
Royal Navy Officers and Ratings, 1803-1856	ADM 13/103-104
Royal Navy Officers and Ratings, and Royal Marines, 1812-1855	ADM 194/42
Royal Navy Officers, 1857-1915	ADM 194/43-45
Royal Navy and Royal Marines, 1911 onwards	ADM 156

Letter Books

Adjutant-General RM's Letter Books: to Woolwich Division, February 1868 to January 1869	ADM 57/1
to Woolwich Division, February to April 1869[1]	ADM 57/2

Regulations

Index to Regulations, 1826-1869	ADM 81/26

See also **Miscellaneous Records**

3.7 MISCELLANEOUS RECORDS

The Attestations and Discharge Certificates in this group may contain records belonging to the Deal Depot, the Royal Marine Artillery and the Woolwich Division.

Miscellaneous Attestations, 1869-1883 (by enlistment)	ADM 157/616-659
Miscellaneous Attestations, 1884-1901 (by discharge)	ADM 157/660-663
Miscellaneous Attestations, 1883-1925 (by discharge)	ADM 157/2058-2303
Miscellaneous Discharge Certificates, 1761-1843	ADM 193/18

[1] Mainly blank. ADM 57/2 and ADM 81/1-9 were rebound while still in the custody of the Royal Marine Office. The two record classes then formed a single series, and ADM 57/2 was lettered on the outside as volume 10.

Description Books, 1755-1803[1]	ADM 158/1-6
Certificates of Continuous Service, [1847-1872]	ADM 157/2304-2407
List of Royal Marines who purchased their discharge, 1818-1824	ADM 6/406
Seniority Lists of Warrant Officers, 1869-1883	ADM 118/212-229
Sheerness Royal Marines' Church, baptisms, 1866-1921	ADM 6/437

3.8 ROYAL MARINE UNITS SERVING OVERSEAS

Although the administrative organization of the Royal Marines remained founded upon the Division, for the purposes of overseas campaigns temporary Brigades and Battalions were formed. Their records are as follows.

IRELAND

Ireland Battalion: Order Book, 1880-1881	ADM 183/39

MEDITERRANEAN

Special Battalion of the Royal Marines Light Infantry, Formed for Service in the Mediterranean: Quartermaster's Diary, 1882	**ADM 183/70**

CHINA

1st Brigade, Canton: List of Promotions and Letter Book, 1859	ADM 193/11
China: Papers, 1840-1902	ADM 201/40-43

SOUTH AFRICA

South Africa Battalion, 1879:

Letter Book	ADM 194/14
Order Book	ADM 183/38
Muster Roll	ADM 193/13

[1] These Description Books provide an haphazard coverage of several Divisions, but mostly of Chatham Division.

NORTHERN AFRICA

2nd Battalion, Suez:

Order Book, 1884-1885	ADM 193/15

RMLI, Suakin and Sudan:

Order Book, 1885	ADM 193/16

Suakin:

Papers, 1884-1885	ADM 201/46-49

Ashanti:

Papers,1873-1874	ADM 201/39

OTHER OVERSEAS POSTS

Overseas Posts:

Papers, 1809-1878	ADM 201/38
Esquimault: Papers, 1883-1896	ADM 201/44

JAPAN

Japan:

Papers, 1862-1875	ADM 201/45

RM Japan Battalion:

Court Martial Registers,1864-1865	ADM 194/41

3.9 LETTER BOOKS AND ORDER BOOKS COVERING ALL DIVISIONS

Adjutant-General RM's Divisional Letter Books, 1806-1867	ADM 56/1-107
Adjutant-General RM's Divisional Letter Books, 1871-1884	ADM 63/1-12
RM Office: Letter Book containing correspondence with War Office and RM Divisions, 1868-1869	ADM 200/1
RM Office: Brigade Order Book; Correspondence with Commandants of Divisions; and In-Letters from Divisions,1831-1838	ADM 201/1

3.10 CORRESPONDENCE BETWEEN ROYAL MARINE OFFICE AND ADMIRALTY

Entry Books, Letters to Admiralty 1862-1868	ADM 191/1-27
Entry Books, Minutes to Admiralty 1862-1868	ADM 191/28-32
Entry Books, Letters and Minutes to Admiralty, 1868-1869	ADM 181/33-34
Entry Books, Submissions to Secretary of the Admiralty, 1869-1875	ADM 191/35-39
Letters from Inspector-General, RM, mostly to Admiralty, 1862-1868	ADM 201/3
Inspector-General RM's Reports and Minutes to Admiralty, 1862-1868	ADM 201/5
Numbers of all ranks of the Royal Marines available for mobilization, 1898	ADM 201/52
Returns of RMs entered, discharged, deserted, etc, 1898-1900	ADM 201/53
Returns to Admiralty, 1869-1881	ADM 201/70
Returns of numbers of officers, warrant and non-commissioned officers, and men ashore and afloat, 1884-1898	ADM 201/71

4. PAY AND ACCOUNTS

4.1 Pay

4.1.1 General

Information about the costs of the Marine Regiments in the early days will be found in the Declared Accounts (Navy) of the Audit Office, 1664 to 1827 (AO 1/1711, roll 105, to AO 1/1783, roll 296). For example, for the costs of the Two Regiments in 1690, the information is in AO 1/1720, roll 135.

Judicious use of the indexes to the Calendars of Treasury Board Papers will alert you to the whereabouts of claims against the Treasury, arrears in payments and salary, estimates and costs associated with the Marines. A full set of calendars of Treasury Board records is available on open access shelves in the lobby at Kew. They are held, too, by the British Library and major research libraries.

Periodic Returns to Parliament, together with Estimates of expenditure for the Royal Navy, the Army and the Marines, are to be found among the published House of Lords and House of Commons papers, of which complete runs are held by the PRO under the references ZHL 1 and ZHC 1 respectively[1]. They should also be available at the House of Lords Record Office, the British Library and major research libraries.

The ultimate paymaster is, of course, HM Treasury. However, the records of the Board of Treasury, insofar as they have survived, are limited in scope. Moreover, they leave you with a somewhat less than favourable impression. The Calendars will point you in the right direction. I commence this analysis with records from the middle years of the eighteenth century. It is nearly always a matter of arrears of pay, such as the communication from Thomas Corbett, Secretary to the Admiralty, addressed to John Scrope, Secretary to the Treasury, concerning the pay of the Marines in Newfoundland, 15 March 1746 (T 1/321/52). That was followed on 11 May 1746 by a letter from Sir William Yonge, Secretary at War, to John Scrope on the matter of the pay of the Marine Regiments (T 1/322/22).

4.1.2 Arrears from 1748

The reorganization of the Marines in 1748 left many financial matters unsettled and major arrears in pay outstanding: the difficulties resulting are documented in surviving Treasury Board records over the subsequent twenty years and more. On 13 June 1749 H Fox, Secretary at War, addressed a memorial to Lord Selwyn on the matter of allowances paid to Marine (T 1/335/47). Fox's letter to John Scrope, Secretary of the Treasury, on 18 March 1752, proposing a method of clearing the accounts of the late Marine Regiments by checking them against the Muster Rolls, is extant (T 1/350/32). But perhaps the method he proposed did not function as smoothly as hoped, for, a year later, on 17 February 1753, we find a warrant for passing the Muster Rolls even though

---

[1] At present, there is a delay of at least twenty-four hours in the production of ZHL 1 volumes for researchers at Kew. Some ZHC 1 volumes are available on microfilm.

they lacked the signature of two commissioned officers (T 1/351/5). Two years later, there were still debts outstanding. On 16 April 1755 the Commissioners of the Navy wrote to George Dodington, Secretary to the Navy, requesting him to obtain from Treasury payment of the arrears that would fall due to the officers of Marine on 31 December 1755 (T 1/366/9).

On 18 October 1759 Viscount Barrington, Secretary at War, wrote to James West, Secretary to the Treasury, sending him a memorial of the field officers and captains of the Late Regiments of Marines (T 1/379/59). On 12 February 1761 Edmund Herbert, Deputy Paymaster of Marines, still had to transmit to Treasury reports concerning the accounts of the disbanded Marine Regiments (T 1/409/231-238). Herbert's case was to have a long run, for on 14 February 1765 Thomas Farraine, the Deputy Auditor, wrote to the Treasury stressing Herbert's desire to settle his accounts separately from those of the other paymasters of the Ten Marine Regiments disbanded in 1748, and enclosing a Treasury Warrant on difficulties incurred by the agents of the disbanded regiments in settling accounts with the Paymaster General of Marines (T 1/437/13-16). On 2 May 1765 Herbert had once more occasion to write to the Treasury on the matter of the settlement of the accounts of those same Ten Regiments (T 1/443/54-59). And yet again, on 9 October 1767 Herbert found himself obliged to memorialize HM Treasury on their behalf, requesting settlement of the regimental accounts (T 1/458/268-270). Later that year, further problems arose, eliciting a memorial from Herbert for a stay of the process against the executors of the late Sir Charles Hanbury Williams regarding the accounts of the Marine Regiments (T 1/462/13 and 14). I have not been able to discover the conclusion to that twenty year struggle with HM Treasury.

4.1.3 Paymasters

Records concerning Marine Paymasters, January 1798 to August 1882, are in ADM 201/26.

4.1.4 Paymasters' Agents

Of organizational interest is the Order in Council authorizing the proposals contained in a memorial from the Commissioners of the Admiralty on the appointment and pay of three agents to serve under the Paymaster of Marines, 17 October 1755 (T 1/371/68).

4.1.5 Half Pay and Allowances

Records of half pay and allowances to reduced officers of the Marines, 25 December 1758 to 24 December 1827, are among the Declared Accounts (Army) of the Audit Office (AO 1/257, roll. 896, to AO 1/261, roll 921).

Records of half pay and allowances to reduced officers of the Marines for 1767 are in T 1/454/223 to 226 (2 copies); comparisons between the state of affairs in 1766 and 1767 are in T 1/454/227 and 228 (2 copies).

The Half Pay Cash Books of the Marine Pay Office, 1763 to 1827, are in ADM 96/87-94. For the years 1822 to 1826, the Half Pay Posting Book has survived (ADM 96/95). The Half Pay Remittance Books from 1808 to 1827 are in ADM 96/96.

4.1.6 Retired Pay

Records of Royal Marine officers' retired pay for the years 1810 to 1820 have survived, and are in ADM 96/102. Thereafter, there is a gap in the records until the period 1871 to 1923 (ADM 22/475 -487).

4.1.7 Recruiting

An Order in Council signed on 1 March 1757 authorized the raising of thirty companies of Marines (T 1/376/24). Recruiting costs money. And so, in May 1757 William Russell, Attorney, Clerk to the Commissioners for Recruiting Land Forces and Marines in Basingstoke and Kingsclere, Hampshire, sent in his claim for expenses (T 1/377/31). Was that claim unique? Or is its survival exceptional? The Recruiting Ledgers of the Marine Pay Office, 1799 to 1830, are in ADM 96/43-49.

4.1.8 Parity with Other Services

In 1883 a committee was set up to recommend on the pay and service conditions of officers of the Royal Marines who were appointed to the General Staff of the Army (WO 33/41, p 41). That same paper contains a report concerning Royal Marines on the permanent staff of the Militia.

A report on the Territorial Depots of the Royal Artillery and the Royal Marine Artillery, 1883, is in WO 33/41, p 935.

4.1.9 Personal Financial Prospects

In 1898 a report was commissioned showing the financial prospects of a Non-Commissioned Officer, from enlistment to discharge (ADM 201/51). Such information helps us to envisage the quality of life of a Royal Marine towards the end of the nineteenth century.

4.1.10 Royal Marines Savings Bank

Records concerning the Royal Marines' Savings Bank, 1825 to 1868, are in ADM 201/33; records for the years 1843 to 1867 are in ADM 201/34-36.

4.1.11 Pay and Service Conditions of Officers, 1883

The records of the work of the Committee on the Pay and Service Conditions of the Royal Marine Officers appointed to the General Staff and employed on the permanent staff of the Volunteer Forces, 1883, are in WO 32/6277[1] (under codes 39A and 59A) and in WO 33/41, p 93.

---

[1] Formerly WO 32/230.

4.1.12 Twentieth-Century Pay Records

Pay records of the present century for the Royal Marines are not always specifically identified in the lists. The Ministry of Defence has tended to subsume records concerning the pay of all branches of the Armed Services under a single designation, all the more in evidence with the development of the concept of combined services.

4.2 Accounts

Among the records of the Marine Pay Office are those of the General Accounts of the Marines for the years 1695 and 1696 (ADM 96/50) and 1702 to 1711 (ADM 96/51). The General Ledgers, 1711 to 1830 (with some years missing) are in ADM 96/31-42. Yearly Accounts registers have survived for the period 1791 to 1818 (ADM 96/52-59). Regimental accounts survive for the 1740s, but in very haphazard manner (ADM 96/69-86). For the Divisions, there are the Divisional Accounts, 1794-1798: Chatham (ADM 96/95), Plymouth (ADM 96/60), Portsmouth (ADM 96/61) and Woolwich (ADM 96/111). The Quartermaster's Accounts, 1819 to 1831, are in ADM 96/114 -116.

5. MILITARY OPERATIONS AND REORGANIZATION IN THE TWENTIETH CENTURY

5.1 Introduction

In operations, the Royal Marines were usually part of a larger fighting unit; and that makes the search for records concerning their part in the operations somewhat difficult. That difficulty becomes particularly acute as the century wore on and the emphasis in military strategy moved in the direction of the complex structures of Combined Operations and Task Forces. Insofar as Royal Marines served on board ship, the ship's records should be searched. Those records include, in general, the ship's log, the captain's report, the convoy report, Naval war diaries, and so on; in other words, a fairly thorough search of Royal Naval records. Records of Combined Operations will likewise reveal details of actions in which Royal Marines were involved. Of course, no explicit mention of Royal Marines will usually appear in the rather brief wording of the record class lists, so that a search among the records mentioned will either be speculative or else prompted by precise information about places, dates and units already in the your possession.

General Standing Orders have survived for 1893 to 1905 (ADM 64/1 and 2), for 1910 to 1922 (ADM 64/3 and 4) and for 1930 to 1942 (ADM 64/135). **General Orders and Instructions** have survived, with some years missing, for the period 1888 to 1936 (ADM 64/5-34). **Circulars and General Instructions** for January 1939 to January 1941 are in ADM 64/35-95. **Routine Orders**, January 1941 to 1963 (indexed for 1947 and 1948), are in ADM 64/96-134.

5.2 War Diaries

5.2.1 First World War

War Diaries, properly so called, are a phenomenon that is first met with during the First World War. For earlier accounts of military and naval engagements, one searches the commanders' despatches to the Admiralty or to the War Office. At the time of the Boer War, it was found that many officers were keeping private journals, often containing very vivid descriptions of the military engagements in which they were taking part, and containing just as often vivid descriptions of life in South Africa at the turn of the century. The military authorities were not slow to perceive the value of those journals, and many were handed in, later to be deposited in the PRO. Surviving War Diaries can be found in ADM 116 and ADM 137. Both classes are comprehensive and fully indexed. They include for example, among the records of the 63rd (Royal Naval) Division, the War Diaries and Operational Orders of the Royal Marine Artillery Howitzer Brigade, August 1915 to December 1916, and the Royal Marine Anti-Aircraft Brigade, December 1915 to January 1916 (ADM 137/3072). Also the Royal Marine Artillery Howitzer Brigade, January 1918 to June 1919, and the 6th Royal Marine Battalion, August 1919 (ADM 137/3073). Others are to be found among Army War Diaries in WO 95. For example, WO 95/4290 and 4291 contain the diaries of the Headquarters of the Royal Marine Brigade, February to August 1915, and the Chatham Battalion, February to July 1915.

5.2.2 Second World War

War Diaries compiled by Royal Marine units during the Second World War will be found in record class ADM 202, arranged by unit, ship or operation code name, as appropriate. It is perfectly clear, from an investigation of the class list, that what has survived is only a small part of what must have been created. In the case of Royal Marine commando units, the diaries should be compared with those in record class DEFE 2, which to some extent duplicate them.

Special Reports of certain campaigns were prepared. Major-General ED Watson's despatch concerning the Sudan Area, Crete, April to May 1941, is in ADM 202/442. The Summaries of Events and Conditions, prepared by the Fleet Royal Marines Officer, Home Fleet, November 1940, December 1941, and March 1943, are in ADM 202/443. The Monthly Letters for May 1941, August 1942, and February 1943, of the Fleet Royal Marines Officer, are in ADM 202/445. The Special Report prepared by the Officer Commanding, concerning the North African Operations Headquarters, November 1942, is in ADM 202/447.

Another group of records, which form an informative ensemble, consists of the **Divisional Despatches**: Chatham Division, November 1940 to April 1941, and September 1941 to June 1943 (ADM 202/435); Portsmouth Division, October 1940 to March 1941, and October 1941 (ADM 202/436); and Plymouth Division, November 1940 to April 1941 (ADM 202/437). There is a summary of the despatches of all three divisions, April 1939 to October 1940, in ADM 202/438. With them is a report on the Reserve Depot at Exmouth, October 1941 to March 1941 (ADM 202/329), together with two other reports: the Mobile Naval Base Defence Organization, June 1941, November 1942, and April to September 1943 (ADM 202/440); and the Siege Regiment, June 1940 to August 1941, and March 1943 to September 1944 (ADM 202/441).

Reports of Service of Royal Marine detachments **on board named HM ships** (including HMNZ ships) in 1945, prepared by the Fleet Royal Marines Office, British Pacific Fleet, are in ADM 202/329-348.

Reports of the Royal Marines' contributions to operations in Europe and the Far East, from 1940 to 1945, are in ADM 202/349-434. The reports are arranged under the code names of the various operations and their dates.

War Diaries that are clearly identified as having been created by units of the Royal Marines during the Second World War, are as follows.

1 (Royal Marines) Commando	DEFE 2/48 1 October 1943 to 30 May 1944	
40 (Royal Marines) Commando	DEFE 2/48 1 December 1943 to 30 September 1945	ADM 202/87 Feb 1942 to Sept 1945
41 (Royal Marines) Commando	DEFE 2/48 10 October 1942 to 30 December 1945	

42 Royal Marines) Commando	DEFE 2/48 1 August 1943 to 31 December 1945	ADM 202/38-41 July 1940; Sept to Dec 1940 ADM 202/94 Aug 1943 to Nov1946
43 (Royal Marines) Commando	DEFE 2/49 1 August 1943 to 31 August 1945	ADM 202/50-53 April 1940 to July 1943 ADM 202/88 Aug 1943 to Aug 1945
44 (Royal Marines) Commando	DEFE 2/50 1 August 1943 to 31 December 1945	ADM 202/54-57 Dec 1939 to July 1943 ADM 202/95-97 Aug 1943 to Nov 1946
45 (Royal Marines) Commando	DEFE 2/51 27 September 1943 to 19 March 1946	ADM 202/42-45 May 1940 to July 1943 ADM 202/81-84 Aug 1943 to Dec 1946
46 (Royal Marines) Commando	DEFE 2/51 1 August 1943 to 31 December 1944	ADM 202/61 Jan 1942 to July 1943
47 (Royal Marines) Commando	DEFE 2/52 1 August 1943 to January 1946	ADM 202/108 Jan to 31 Mar, Aug, December 1944 ADM 202/109 Jan to Dec 1945 ADM 202/110 Jan 1946
48 (Royal Marines) Commando	DEFE 2/52 2 March 1944 to 30 November 1945	ADM 202/65 Jan to Mar 1944 ADM 202/111 Mar to Dec1944 ADM 202/112 Jan to Nov1945

Royal Marines Engineer Commando	DEFE 2/49 2 February 1944 to 30 November 1945	
Royal Marines Section, General Headquarters, 2nd Echelon, 21st Army Group	DEFE 2/53 10 April 1944 to 17 December 1945	ADM 202/10 May 1943 ADM 202/77 Oct 1943 to Nov 1944; Jan to Dec 1945

5.2.3 Korean War

The war diaries of Royal Marine contingents to the United Nations forces are to be found in record class ADM 202, which covers the years 1939 to 1964. The United Nations Command Reports, in DEFE 12/1-39, cover the period July 1950 to 11 September 1955. The records of the complements of HM ships, compiled for the Director General, Naval Manpower, 1952 to 1969, are in record class ADM 299.

5.2.4 The Falklands War and the Persian Gulf War

No official records of the two conflicts are yet open to public inspection. That being so, you are advised to consult the newspaper reports and officers' memoirs for information about the part played by the Royal Marines. Newspapers are held at the

British Library
Newspaper Library
Colindale Avenue
LONDON
NW9 5HE,

which is open to *bona fide* researchers in possession of a valid British Library reader's ticket. The Royal Marines' magazine, *The Globe and Laurel*, not held by the PRO, contains some very informative articles and photographs.

The researcher today has, in fact, available the resources of the press, radio and video with computer-aided enhancement as never before. The technology for the latter is now at such a level of sophistication that highly detailed photographs could be transmitted back to Britain, passing through computerized censoring on the way, so that they could be published immediately. The press has gained, too, interviews with the commanding officers, who at times revealed strategy and spoke their minds with enough clarity to annoy the powers-that-be. In the case of the multi-national force, differing interpretations of official secrecy have already put a fairly balanced statement before researchers. As a consequence, it has become difficult to imagine what the war diaries, once released to public scrutiny, will be able to add to our knowledge of the campaigns.

5.3 Miscellaneous Papers of the Second World War Period

5.3.1 Second World War Establishment Records

War Establishment records of the **Royal Marine Division**, 1941 to 1943, are in DEFE 2/888. Records of war establishment matters of N° 3 Commando Brigade, Royal Marines, Hong Kong, 1947 and 1948, are in DEFE 2/1469. The proposed war establishments for Commando units, Royal Marines, 1946, is in DEFE 2/1730. Miscellaneous correspondence concerning the organization, employment and training of Royal Marines, 1942 to 1947, is in DEFE 2/984.

A statement of the Royal Marines' requirements in the future Combined Operations Headquarters, 1949, is in DEFE 2/1717.

5.3.2 Royal Marines Commandos

The records of the formation and reorganization of the Royal Marines Commandos, 1943 and 1944, are in DEFE 2/1041. The records of the restructuring of the Royal Marines and of the Royal Marines Commandos, 1961 to 1964, are in DEFE 13/159.

5.3.3 Royal Marines Boom Patrol Detachment

The records of the formation of the Royal Marines Boom Patrol Detachment, 1942 to 1944, are in DEFE 2/953. Reports of the Detachment's operations, 1942 to 1944, are in DEFE 2/952, and historical records of the Detachment, 1942 to 1948, are in DEFE 2/988.

5.4 Post-War Organization and Training

5.4.1 Ministry of Defence Records

Records concerning the post-war policy, the organization and training of the Royal Marines Commandos, 1945 and 1946, are in DEFE 2/1336.

A file created during 1946 and 1947, on the Command and Organization of Royal Marine Commandos, contains proposals for the reorganization of the Royal Marines in the United Kingdom under the command of the Commandant General, RM, and their approval by the Board (DEFE 2/1494).

The post-war years initially saw the reduction of the armed services, reductions that were not without their effect upon the strength of the Royal Marines, until the evolution of the Cold War required the maintenance of a significant defence capability. It has been only in the Gorbachev and Yeltsin years that the spectre of major war, which has haunted Europe since 1945, is being laid to rest.

The centre of potential hostilities has, in the meantime, moved. Threats against Britain's sovereignty, or against the sovereignty of countries with which Britain is treaty-bound, have appeared in the Southern Atlantic Ocean and Mesopotamia. The Royal Marines played a major role in the Falklands War and again in the multi-national force that the United Nations directed against the invader of Kuwait. Official reports of those campaigns are still too recent to be publicly available. However, the general shift in Defence thinking and planning is becoming clear in outline to all observers: a development of quick response task forces within a framework of combined operations. The most recent documentation bearing upon that evolution with respect to the Royal Marines will be closed to public inspection for at least a period of thirty years.

Planning for the post-war armed services began during the closing stages of the Second World War. The records of that planning are among the records of Combined Operations (DEFE), of the Admiralty (ADM) and of the Cabinet (CAB) and Prime Minister's Office (PREM). You are warned, however, that it is by no means always clear, judging uniquely by its official title, whether a given document will contain information concerning the Royal Marines. Those files that carry a clear reference to Royal Marines pose, of course, no problem of identification; but they are comparatively rare. On the other hand, the words 'Combined Operations' in a document's title should be taken as indicating the likelihood that it contains information relative to the Royal Marines in the context of other or all branches of the armed services. The next clue that should alert you is a reference to a locality or to a date or to an operation significant for Royal Marines' activities.

Of particular significance for our understanding of the evolution of the Royal Marines in the post-war period are the records concerning the new structures of the Royal Marines and of the Royal Marines Commandos, 1961 to 1964 (DEFE 13/159). You may find it worth while scrutinizing any file in the description of which there is reference to 'joint-services' or 'inter-services', despite the absence of any specific mention of Royal Marines. Such expressions reflect the doctrine of Combined Operations. Some obvious such records are those concerning the review of pay and conditions arising from meetings among all service departments, 1954 and 1955, in DEFE 13/27. Records of the rationalization of medical services throughout the Armed Forces, 1960 to 1964, should contain matters of interest to students of Royal Marine records. On medical matters, there are also the records concerning the recruitment of doctors for HM Forces, 1962 (DEFE 13/256). The records of the Inter-Services Staff Colleges, 1857 to 1961, are in DEFE 13/175. Finally, we note the Registered Files of the Chiefs of Staff Committee, in record class DEFE 11, and the descriptions of files there concerning joint-services planning. Such a search will be, of course, speculative.

5.4.2 Cabinet Office Records

The Armed Forces are ultimately responsible to Parliament through the Minister of Defence. Consequently, investigations among the records left by the Cabinet Office (record classes CAB) should prove fruitful. Those records have excellent indexes and means of cross-reference. Classes of particular interest in the present context include the following, although you should be aware that some files are subject to a fifty year closure period or even retention by the office of origin.

CAB 55: Committee of Imperial Defence, Joint Planning Committee, 1923 to 1939 (the class is continued in CAB 84 and CAB 119).

CAB 56: Committee of Imperial Defence, Joint Intelligence Committee, 1936 to 1974.

CAB 65: War Cabinet Minutes, 1939 to 1945.

CAB 66, CAB 67 and CAB 68: War Cabinet Memoranda, covering, among them, the years 1939 to 1945.

CAB 69: War Cabinet Defence Committee (Operations), 1940 to 1945.

CAB 84: War Cabinet Planning Committee, 1939 to 1947.

CAB 119: Joint Planning Staff, 1939 to 1948 (continuing CAB 55 and CAB 84).

CAB 120: Minister of Defence, Secretariat Files, 1938 to 1947.

CAB 122: British Joint Staff Missions: Washington Office Files, 1940 to 1958.

CAB 128: Cabinet Minutes, 1945 to 1960.

CAB 129: Cabinet Memoranda, 1945 to 1962.

CAB 131: Defence Committee (continuing CAB 69 and CAB 70), 1946 to 1961.

CAB 138: British Joint Staff Missions: Correspondence and Papers (to be supplemented with items in CAB 80, CAB 88 and CAB 122), 1942 to 1975.

CAB 140: Official Historians' Correspondence, 1942 to 1958.

5.4.3 Defence Council Records

Among the Formal Documents of the Defence Council are the Directions of the Defence Council to to the Admiralty Board: Admiralty Board Directions. Those particular documents are of special historical or military significance. Although dated 28 April 1978, the file is open to public inspection (DEFE 17/1). You may also find interesting the file concerning the reconstitution of the Defence Council, dated 28 April 1978, but open to public inspection (DEFE 17/4). Of possible interest in respect of combined operations developments is the report of the inquiry into Naval Carrier Task Forces, 1962 to 1965 (DEFE 19/20) which is not yet available to the public.

5.5 Miscellaneous Units

5.5.1 Amphibian Support Regiment, Royal Marines

The records of the organization and training of the 34th Amphibian Support Regiment, Royal Marines, together with an account of its move to India and return to Braunston Camp, Barnstaple, 1944 to 1946, are in DEFE 2/1286.

5.5.2 Amphibious School, Royal Marines

The records of the establishment of the Amphibious School, Royal Marines, Portsmouth, and the functions of the Beach Wing, the organization of basic training in small Wing Raids, directives to the Commandant, Amphibious School, RM, 1946 to 1948, are in DEFE 2/1619. A report issued by the Commandant, Amphibious School, Royal Marines, on trials of beach signs, 1950, is in DEFE 2/1498. The report was made in the context of the considerable discussion on beach signs in Combined Operations at the time.

5.5.3 Amphibious Warfare Experimental Establishment (AWEE)

The records comprise the directive, outstanding orders and financial arrangements for the AWEE, and the proposed amalgamation with Amphibious School, Royal Marines, 1953 (DEFE 2/1830).

5.5.4 Royal Marines Signal School

The proposal for an amalgamation of the Royal Marines Signal School, Eastney, with the Combined Signal School, Fremington, 1950, is in DEFE 2/1863.

5.5.5 Special Boat Section, Royal Marines (SBS, RM)

The narrative of the Special Boat Section and the records of the proposal to use the title 'Special Boat Section' (SBS) for part of the Royal Marines, 1950 and 1951, are in DEFE 2/1621. A file created during 1954 and 1955 contains information concerning the roles and organization of the SBS, and the requirements for the unit in the Mediterranean, together with a record of the Exercise code-named 'Drake's Drum' (DEFE 2/1907). In 1956 it was proposed that the Clearance Diving Team (Amphibious) should be taken over by the SBS, RM (DEFE 2/1908).

5.5.6 N° 3 Commando Brigade, Royal Marines

There is a report on special equipment requirements for N° 3 Commando Brigade, Royal Marines, together with Routine Orders, and an account of the presentation of a silver salver from the Government of Hong Kong, 1947 and 1948, in DEFE 2/1469. For the same unit, there are records of war establishment matters, the responsibility for the movement of drafts to and fro, together with the minutes of a conference on the special equipment requirements of the unit, 1950, in DEFE 2/1470.

The operational records and the quarterly newsletters of N° 3 Commando Brigade, Royal Marines, 1952 to 1954, are in DEFE 2/1836, but closed to public inspection for a period of fifty years.

5.5.7 N° 41 (Royal Marines) Commando

The records of the inquiry raised by Viscountess Davidson MP in 1945, regarding the recognition and awards of N° 41 (Royal Marines) Commando, are in DEFE 2/1295.

5.5.8 N° 46 (Royal Marines) Commando

A history of the N° 46 (Royal Marines) Commando, covering the years 1942 to 1945, is in DEFE 2/977.

5.6 Co-operation between Royal Marines and United States Marine Corps

Discussions took place, in 1951, between Headquarters' staff, Amphibious Warfare, and a United States of America Marine Corps School visiting Great Britain. A summary and the minutes of the meeting are in DEFE 2/1822. Records of the appointment of a representative from the United States' Marine Corps for Amphibious Warfare Centre, Fremington, together with a study of American and British techniques, are in DEFE 2/1841.

6. CEREMONIES AND WAR MEMORIALS

6.1 Ceremonies

Most records concerning ceremonial are likely to be found in private papers and especially in the Orders of the Day and the mess books. They are not in the custody of the Public Record Office, but some are held in the Royal Marines Museum and Library, Eastney, and others in the Portsmouth Record Office[1]. Records of ceremonies for which special permission was required have, on the other hand, been deposited in the PRO, and include those relative to the lighting of the King's Candlestick in Royal Marines officers' messes, 1949 to 1960 (ADM 201/107), the presentation of the new Colours to the Royal Marines Barracks, Eastney, by HRH the Duke of Edinburgh, on St George's Day, 23 April 1956 (ADM 201/108), and the drinking of Loyal Toasts, 1953 to 1971 (ADM 201/116, not yet open for public inspection).

6.2 War Memorials

Records concerning the Combined Operations Memorial, a stained glass window for the Chapel of the Royal Naval College, Dartmouth, 1943, 1944 and 1947, are in DEFE 2/1592. Records dated 1949 to 1951, concerning war memorials to Royal Naval and Royal Marine personnel, are in ADM 201/103. Records concerning the ceremonial opening of the Corporal Tom Hunter, VC, RM, Memorial Cottages, 1952 to 1954, are in ADM 201/105.

---

[1]Cf A J Lowe (editor), *Records of the Portsmouth Division of Marines, 1764-1800* (Portsmouth Record Series, 7), Portsmouth, 1990

7. MEDICAL, EDUCATIONAL AND MUSICAL RECORDS

7.1 Hospital Records

7.1.1 Hospital Records of Eighteenth and Nineteenth Centuries

Hospital Musters covering the years 1740 to 1869 are in record class ADM 102. The Establishment Book of the Royal Marine Infirmary at Woolwich, 1817 to 1820, is in ADM 104/3.

7.1.2 Hospital Records of the First World War

A selection of hospital admission and discharge registers, 2nd General Hospital, for Royal Marines, 1918, is to be found in MH 106/986-997. Sick and wounded were admitted to dressing stations and hospitals irrespective of the branch of service, so that speculative searches should be widely based. The war diaries of Army hospitals are in record class WO 95. Records of evacuation by hospital ships are in record class WO 222.

The service records of the members of the Royal Marine Medical Unit, 1914 to 1918, are in ADM 159/209 and 210. There are no indexes to them in ADM 313, where one might well have expected to find them.

7.1.3 Hospital Records of the Second World War

War Diaries of Army hospitals should be searched (WO 169). Records of selected hospital ships are in the Medical Historian's papers in record class WO 222. The War Diaries of hospital ships are in WO 171/1414-1450.

7.1.4 Medical and Hospital Records of the post Second World War period

The post-war years witnessed the winding down of the armed services, with a flow-on effect upon the medical services branches. Another important phenomenon, that should always be kept in mind in searching for medical records belonging to the period, is the evolution of Combined Forces Operations: the surviving records will often contain all or much of what in former times would have been discrete to the records of a given service branch. Sometimes it is clear from the description of a document that a particular service is more concerned than another; and I have tried to select those that appear to have more specifically to do with Royal Marines than with others. In fact, any record pertaining to joint-services could well contain information concerning the Royal Marines. For example, the minutes and memoranda of the Working Party on Medical Establishments in the Services, 1947, are apposite (DEFE 10/91). And so are the records of the Medical

Services Co-ordinating Committee and Standing Sub-Committees, 1948 to 1951 (DEFE 10/92-95).

Records (including a map) concerning the establishment of a Royal Marines Service Hospital in the Near East, 1958 to 1963, are in DEFE 7/1778. The records of the medical arrangements made for Royal Marines at SHAPE and Fontainebleau, 1952 to 1959, are in DEFE 7/322-332; those concerning the arrangements at SHAPE, Fontainebleau and at the British Hospital in Paris, 1962 and 1963, are in DEFE 7/1861. The papers and minutes of the Forces Medical and Dental Services Committee (the Lord Waverley Committee), 1953 to 1962, are in DEFE 7/333-359.

7.2 Royal Marines Schools and Teachers

Records of Royal Marines Schools and of Royal Marines teachers, 1840 to 1890, are in ADM 201/37. Children of servicemen of all services attend the school on base or the nearest to base, whether Army or Royal Navy. A speculative search through Routine Orders may provide information about schools, schoolchildren, curriculum and teachers. Such records for the Army provide at times a considerable volume of detail (WO 123).

7.3 Royal Marine Bands and Music

Since 1917, the Band of the Royal Marines has provided the music not only for the Corps but also for the Royal Navy. The band school is located at the depot at Deal. Very few records concerning the band have survived. A file, prepared between 1955 and 1957, concerns the terms of employment of music tutors at the Royal Marines School of Music (ADM 201/113). Records concerning the training of Junior Musicians at the Royal School of Music and the creation of the Commandant-General Royal Marines Squad, 1948 to 1958, are in DEFE 201/117. The Report of the Leech-Porter Committee on the formation of a Royal Marine Band Service, 1949, is in ADM 201/121. Records concerning the emergency operational roles for the Royal Marine Band Service and its employment in action, 1958 to 1967, are in ADM 201/118 (not yet open to public inspection). The 'Redeployment Plan', a review of the employment of Royal Marine Bands and Bandsmen, 1956 to 1959, is in ADM 201/119.

The present day, official march of the Royal Marines is the march of the Preobrazhensky Regiment of the Russian Imperial Guards. During the Peninsular Wars, it had been the march of the Grenadier Guards: the confusion that it, coupled with the wearing of the Grenadier bonnet (then part of the Marines' uniform), created in the minds of the enemy is told in private papers and recounted in standard histories.

The service records of Royal Marines Bandsmen, 1903 to 1908, are in ADM 159/103-112.

8. SERVICE RECORDS

8.1 OFFICERS

8.1.1 Publications

Confirmation of a Commission or an appointment of a (Royal) Marine officer can sometimes be ascertained from official publications. The gazetting of a Marine's Commission, promotions and resignation appeared in the *London Gazette*, a monthly publication available in major research libraries: a set is held in the PRO under reference ZJ 1. Although, for the nineteenth and twentieth centuries, every second volume is indexed, the publication is not recommended for a speculative search. Outlines of officers' careers prior to 1793 can often be reconstructed from the information provided about (Royal) Marine officers on full pay and on half pay in the annual published *List of Officers of the (Royal) Marine Forces*: the PRO holds two defective sets, which together cover the period 1757 to 1886 (ADM 118/230-336 for the years 1757 to 1850 [indexed from 1770 onwards]; ADM 192/1-44 for the years 1760 to 1886). Similar information may be obtained from the annually published *Army List* from 1740 onwards, and in the semi-official *Hart's Army List* from 1840 onwards. (Royal) Marines are also listed in the annually published *Navy List* from 1797 onwards, while the semi-official *New Navy List* contains records of Royal Marine officers from 1840, and, from 1846, provides short statements of service (fleshed out sometimes with anecdotal information) reaching back to the last decade of the eighteenth century. Good runs of those publications are available on open access shelves at Kew.

Annual establishment lists of officers of the Marines were compiled for the years 1664 to 1701 and published by L Edye[1]. Manuscript annotations to the annual *Marine Officers' Lists*, in record class ADM 118, appear to be authentic and provide establishment statistics.

8.1.2 Official Records: Prior to 1793

No **Records of Service** of Marine officers appointed prior to 1793 have survived. However, some very brief statements about an officer's commissioning and appointments can be obtained by searching the **Commissions and Appointments Registers** for the years 1703 to 1713 (ADM 6/405), and for the years 1755 to 1814 (ADM 6/406). They are in date order with no nominal index.

Those few years apart, there survives a complete run of **Royal Warrants** for Commissions and Appointments, 1664 to 1854, in State Papers Domestic, Military Entry Books, in record class SP 44, held at Chancery Lane, and in the Military Entry Books of the successor department, viz. the Home Office, Military Entry Books, in record class HO 51, held at Kew. In the older literature, both record classes are somewhat misleadingly referred to by the single designation of Home Office, Military Entry Books. Their numerical sequence is slightly erratic; but the key to their use is as follows.

[1] L. Edye, *The Historical records of the Royal Marines, 1664-1701*, London: Harrison and Sons, 1893 (PRO library reference MN.181).

State Papers Domestic, Military Entry Books

Vol 1	=	SP 44/164	1679 to 1687
Vol 2	=	SP 44/166	1688 to 1693
Vol 3	=	SP 44/167	1690 to 1702
Vol 4	=	SP 44/168	1694 to 1702
Vol 5	=	SP 44/170	1702 to 1704
Vol 6	=	SP 44/171	1702 to 1706
Vol 7	=	SP 44/172	1704 to 1709
Vol 8	=	SP 44/175	1707 to 1714
Vol 9	=	SP 44/173	1706 to 1714
Vol 10	=	SP 44/176	1714 to 1717
Vol 11	=	SP 44/177	1714 to 1723
Vol 12	=	SP 44/178	1717 to 1726
Vol 13	=	SP 44/180	1726 to 1729
Vol 14	=	SP 44/179	1723 to 1731
Vol 15	=	SP 44/181	1726 to 1729
Vol 16	=	SP 44/182	1731 to 1740
Vol 17	=	SP 44/183	1740 to 1743
Vol 18	=	SP 44/184	1740 to 1744
Vol 19	=	SP 44/186	1745 to 1747
Vol 20	=	SP 44/185	1743 to 1747
Vol 21	=	SP 44/187	1747 to 1754
Vol 22	=	SP 44/188	1747 to 1755
Vol 23	=	SP 44/189	1754 to 1758
Vol 24	=	SP 44/191	1758 to 1759
Vol 25	=	SP 44/190	1755 to 1760
Vol 26	=	SP 44/192	1760 to 1762
Vol 27	=	SP 44/194	1760 to 1781
Vol 28	=	SP 44/196	1763 to 1782

Home Office, Military Entry Books

Vol 146	=	HO 51/146	1782 to 1792

The Military Entry Books contain records of the Commissions, promotions and appointments of Army and (Royal) Marine officers, including chaplains and medical officers. On occasions, the full officer establishment of a regiment is stated, particularly in the case of a newly formed or re-formed regiment. Occasionally, too, warrants for the holding of a Court Martial on a named officer are to be found, naming also the Judge Advocate. Some correspondence is included in the Military Entry Books, some of which may be found on closer study to have bearing upon the (Royal) Marines.

Other sources of information that name individual (Royal) Marine officers, are the *House of Commons' Journal*, a run of which is held in the PRO Library at Kew under reference P.4*, and the *House of Lords' Journal* (PRO Library reference P.1*). For instance, volume 13 of the *House of Commons' Journal*, for the year 1689, a year of major reorganization of the Marines, provides references to many Marine officers. You should ask help of the officers on duty in the Reference Room to obtain access to the *Journal*. The latter should be available, too, in the British Library and other major research libraries.

8.1.3 Official Records: Post 1793

For records of **Royal Marine Infantry Officers** commissioned after 1793, a search should begin among the Records of Officers' Service (ADM 196/58-65, 83 and 97-105). In addition to the service information about an officer, those records sometimes provide indications of the name and profession of his father. Note, however, that the first volume of the series (viz ADM 196/58) does not contain short-service records, but only records of those officers who served well into the nineteenth century. Moreover, the coverage is complete only from about 1837. Records in this on-going series are open to public inspection with respect to officers appointed up to the year 1915 (who in some cases saw their last service as late as 1954). Records of **Royal Marine Artillery Officers** for the years 1798 to 1855 (who in some cases served until 1870) are in ADM 196/66. The **Embarkation Books** (WO 25) provide some information about officers embarked on board. They state the ship's name, the officer's name, his rank, his regiment, the dates of his entry and discharge (or death), together with the number of NCOs and men embarked with him.

An alphabetical list of (Royal) Marine officers, whose service record has survived, 1793 to 1970, is contained in ADM 313/110, additional copies of which are available on open access shelves in the Reference Room. It provides the reference in full to the location of the officer's service record in ADM 196. Enquiries concerning officers appointed after 1915 should be addressed to the

Commandant General
Royal Marines
Ministry of Defence (Navy)
Whitehall
LONDON
SW1.

In the case of officers who have died, very comprehensive information concerning their careers may often be found in obituary notices published in *The Times* and in the Royal Marines' magazine, entitled *The Globe and Laurel*. Both are indexed. Neither is an official record, and neither is held by the PRO. Biographies given in privately published lists of gallantry medal winners, although not official records, often provide very full information. The same should be said of the articles in the *Dictionary of National Biography* for high-ranking officers. Some of the medal list publications and a set of the *Dictionary of National Biography* are to be found on open access shelves in the Reference Room at Kew and in some public libraries.

Admiralty Leave Books contain entries for Royal Marine officers as well as for Royal Naval officers, 1804 to 1846 (ADM 6/200-206). The information contained is only of the officers' leave entitlements. It is arranged in date order, and there is no nominal index.

A **Survey of Royal Marines Officers' Ages** was conducted in 1822 (ADM 6/405). For each officer, the survey provides the following information: name, rank, date of seniority, actual age on 1 April 1822, whether in receipt of allowances other than pay, and amount of pay.

Records of **Half pay and Allowances** to reduced officers of the (Royal) Marines, 25 December 1758 to 24 December 1827, are among the Declared Accounts (Army) of the Audit Office (AO 1/257, roll 896, to AO 1/261, roll 921). A list of reduced officers, made in 1801, has survived and is in ADM 96/104. **The Address Book of Reduced Officers** on unattached, retired full pay and (reserved) half pay, 1816, is in ADM 96/511.

There are some **memorials** concerning matters of pay from named officers, 1711 to 1728, in ADM 96/112.

Index Branch Registers for Service Nominations as Lieutenants in the Royal Marine Light Infantry, 1882 to 1892, are in ADM 6/448, and for the years 1891 to 1902, in ADM 6/450. They are the only such registers known to have survived.

Lists of Combined Operations Royal Naval and Royal Marine Officers have survived for 1943 (DEFE 2/762), for 1944 (DEFE 2/1787) and for 1945 (DEFE 2/763).

There is an index to persons mentioned in DEFE 2/781-1373, files covering the period 1937 to 1945, in DEFE 2/1373. Some of those named are Royal Marines.

8.1.4 Individual Cases

The case of Lieutenant Alexander Livingstone, of the Portsmouth Division of Marines, who was mistakenly arrested and maltreated as a Mr Stamford, a debtor, 1766, is fully documented in T 1/455/137-140.

Among the Treasury Office Registered Papers is the memorial of Captain Samuel Hood, asking for appointment to the honorary post of Colonel of Marines as a reward for his distinguished services, of which he provided full details, 1 March 1774 (T 1/504/32 and 33).

A report on the deaths of Lieutenant E A T Wright, RM, and Corporal A W Allen, RM, members of the Swimming Unit of Combined Operations, is included among reports of accidents resulting in the death of personnel, 1943 to 1948, in DEFE 2/1145.

8.2 WARRANT OFFICERS

The sole record of Warrant Officers' service (ADM 196/67) is labelled 'Book II', though no 'Book I' is known to have survived. It is indexed, along with the officers' service records, in ADM 313/110 (copies of which are available on open access shelves in the Reference Room at Kew). It contains information about Royal Marines Warrant Officers appointed between 1904 and 1912 (and serving up to 1923). Few specific records of Warrant Officers' service have been kept. However, as many Warrant Officers went on to become Commissioned Officers, their service records, including information about their service as Warrant Officers, will be found among the records of officers' service.

8.3 ROYAL MARINE CHAPLAINS

The first chaplain appointed to the Marine Regiments was the Reverend John Evans, commissioned on 11 November 1664 (WO 25/1, p 34). Following the reorganization of the Marines in 1672, he was reappointed on [8 July 1673] (SP 44/35A, p 74A). He was succeeded on 1 July 1685 by the Reverend Samuel Morse (SP 44/164, p 238). Morse was present at the Camp on Hounslow Heath on 6 June 1687 (BL Add MSS 9,760) and was still with the Regiment on disbandment in February 1688/9 (AO 1/54, roll 43).

8.3.1 Second Regiment Chaplains

The first chaplain known to have been appointed to the 2nd Regiment was the Reverend Francis Morgan, 17 January 1690 (SP 44/167).

8.3.2 Chaplains who formerly were Marines

There are a number of recorded cases of an officer resigning his commission in order to take Holy Orders, and thereafter returning to the Armed Forces as a Chaplain. One case noted is that of Captain Paul Batchelour, whose name appears on the 'List and Establishment of Half Pay to y[e] Reformed Officers of y[e] Two late Marine Regiments', 20 August 1690 (SP 44/167, p 367), and who subsequently took Holy Orders and was appointed Chaplain to Colonel John Hill's Regiment of Foot, 6 December 1707 (SP 44/172, f 135).

In general records of (Royal) Marine Chaplains are to be expected among the full range of officers' records.

8.4 ROYAL MARINE SURGEONS

The first surgeon to be appointed to the Marines was Simon Boninga, 11 November 1664 (WO 25/1, p 35, where the marginal reading gives Benning). He was present at the first muster on 16 November 1664 (SP 29/110, p 28). He was apparently succeeded by Samuel Tatham, whose commission was dated 11 February 1665 (SP 44/165, p 157), and renewed on 14 September 1666 (WO 25/1, p 220). He was reappointed in October 1684 (SP 44/164), was present at the Camp on Hounslow Heath on 6 June 1687 (BL, Add MSS 9,760), and was still a member of the Regiment at its disbandment in February 1689 (AO 1/54, roll 43).

8.4.1 First Regiment

Following the reorganization of the Marines in 1690, Robert Manesty was appointed surgeon to the First Regiment of Marines, 16 January 1690 (SP 44/166, p 82). He was succeeded by Thomas Pearce on 14 March 1691 (SP 44/167, p 55). In 1694 he gained two Assistant Surgeons, William Blackburne and John Newton. Pearce was succeeded by John Conny on 7 March 1695 (SP 44/168, p 101), the two assistants remaining in office. Conny was still in office in 1698, but we read no more of the Assistant Surgeons after 1696.

8.4.2 Second Regiment

Francis Mogson was appointed surgeon to the Second Regiment of Marine on 17 January 1690 (SP 44/166, p 83). He was replaced by Richard Huckeley on 16 January 1691 (SP 44/167, p 43). Two years later, 1693, two Assistant Surgeons were added to the Regiment's establishment: Roland Fragmore and George Agar (BL Add MSS 9313). Huckeley was succeeded by Henry Worth on 1 April 1694 (SP 44/167, p 194), his assistants still in office. On 13 March 1685 Christopher Robinson succeeded Worth (SP 44/167, p241), and was still in office on 31 December 1698. There is no further mention of the Assistant Surgeons.

A thorough search of State Papers Domestic, Military Entry Books (SP 44), and the War Office Commission Books (WO 25), will prove fruitful. The original registers are indexed, or else the name of the officer and his unit clearly stated in the margin of the page against the commission entry. The Calendars of State Papers too are fully indexed, and will refer you to the original document.

References to Royal Marine Surgeons will be found in the various lists of officers' service records. Among the records of the Admiralty Medical Department will be found the Establishment Book of the Royal Marine Infirmary at Woolwich, 1817 to 1829 (ADM 104/3). Records of personnel of the Royal Marine Medical Unit, 1914 to 1918, are in ADM 159/209 and 210. No index to those records is available, according to a note in the class list of ADM 313.

8.5 OTHER RANKS

8.5.1 Introduction

The basic arrangement of records of other ranks' service is according to Division. If you do not know, or cannot ascertain the Division to which a Marine belonged you will need to search the records of each Division. If you know a Marine's Company Number and service dates, you can ascertain the Division by using the tables set out in the *List of Officers of the (Royal) Marine Forces* for each year (ADM 118 and ADM 192) or in Appendix 1. Generally speaking, a Marine remained for the duration of his service with the Division into which he had enlisted. Moreover, he tended to remain in the Company into which he had enlisted, unless promotion entailed transfer. There is a complicating factor here, to which further research should bring the solution: in the latter years of the nineteenth century, men appear to have been appointed to companies bearing alphabetical designations, then to numerically designated companies. Occasional instances of transfer between Divisions are not easy to account for.

A project is at present under way that will result in the production of a nominal list of all Royal Marines other rankers for whom a record of service has survived, whether Attestation, Description Book entry or Service Record. The list will contain enough information to enable you to identify the man, and will provide the reference or references to the surviving document or documents. It is expected to take several years to complete; and, in the meanwhile, enquiries concerning it should be addressed to the Reader Services Department at Kew.

8.5.2 Attestations (ADM 157)

Two independently created **indexes** to surviving Attestations are in the custody of the PRO. Firstly, there are the official indexes to Attestations in ADM 313/1-26. Secondly, there is available in the Reference Room a nominal index, on filing cards, of nineteenth-century Royal Marines for whom an Attestation has survived. It is intended that the filing cards will, in due time, be superseded by the consolidated list above mentioned.

Attestations (ADM 157) are the loose forms compiled for each Marine on enlistment. They contain personal information, such as birthplace, previous occupation, physical description, sometimes the identification of next of kin, and the full record of the Marine's service. Surviving Attestations are filed by Division and then either by date of enlistment or date of discharge, as shown in the following table. Those filed by date of discharge are normally attached to a document entitled 'Discharge Book', which is the record of the discharge's authenticity. 'Book' is a grand title for a sheet of paper.

Chatham Division

1790 to 1883: by date of enlistment (ADM 157/1-139)

1842 to 1912: by date of discharge (ADM 157/1276-1851)

During the First World War, the Royal Marines accepted short service enlistment for the duration of hostilities. Within that framework, a Royal Marine Labour Corps was established at Chatham, 1915 to 1919. The Attestations for men of the Labour Corps are in ADM 157/3459-3466, and are in numerical order.

Plymouth Division

1804 to 1838: by date of enlistment (ADM 157/140)

1842 to 1883: by date of discharge (ADM 157/141-337)

1842 to 1900: by date of discharge (ADM 157/1852-1868)

Portsmouth Division

1804 to 1836: by date of enlistment (ADM 157/338-352)

1837 to 1883: by date of discharge (ADM 157/353-615)

1869 to 1904: by date of discharge (ADM 157/1869-2057)

1904 to 1923: by date of discharge (ADM 157/2471-2847)

Attestations of Portsmouth Division Royal Marines Other Ranks sequestrated to the Royal Marine Artillery, 1834 and 1835, are in ADM 157/664.

Royal Marine Artillery

Attestations of men of the Royal Marine Artillery were deposited in the PRO according to three distinct systems. In the **first group**, the order is alphabetical, but the chronological coverage is inconsistent:

Surnames beginning A to L, 1865 to 1918: by date of discharge (ADM 157/2848).

Surnames beginning M to Z, 1861 to 1917: by date of discharge (ADM 157/2849).

In the **second group**, the Attestations are arranged in alphabetical order; the numbers stated in the record class list are entirely irrelevant for research, as they simply indicate the number of Attestations contained on each file. The records cover the years 1860 to 1923 (ADM 157/2850-3246).

The **third group** comprises miscellaneous certificates of service arranged in nominal order and covering the period 1899 to 1925 (ADM 157/3247-3269).

Woolwich Division

Woolwich Division existed from 1805 to 1869. The earliest surviving Attestation of a Woolwich Division Royal Marine belongs to the year 1839.

1839 to 1869: by date of discharge (ADM 157/665-1275)

Deal Depot

Deal Depot was reorganized during the First World War as another base for the Royal Marine Labour Corps on short term, or hostilities only, enlistment, 1914 to 1922. Their Attestations are filed in numerical order, 8000 to 15955 (ADM 157/3270-3458).

Royal Marines Engineers: Short Term Attestations

During the First World War, the Royal Marines accepted enlistment for the duration of hostilities. The Attestations of the Royal Marines Engineers in that category, 1914 to 1919, are in numerical order (ADM 157/3467-3625).

Miscellaneous

Miscellaneous Attestations are for those recruits to whom no Official Number was allocated and who served only a matter of days or months at the most.

1869 to 1883: by date of enlistment (ADM 157/616-659)

1884 to 1901: by date of discharge (ADM 157/660-663)

1884 to 1925: by date of discharge (ADM 157/2058-2303)

A miscellaneous group of Certificates of Continuous Service has recently been deposited in the PRO. They are in nominal order and, although dated by the Ministry of Defence to about 1865, a spot check authorizes me to say that this group contains certificates of service that commenced at least as early as 1847 and continued until at least 1872. Further research may well push those limits further apart still. It may also reveal some as belonging to Royal Marines who formerly belonged to the Woolwich Division, which was closed in 1869; but that does not appear to explain the majority of them, since the Division and HM ships or stations are clearly indicated together with the dates of service. In effect, they contain the same service information as that which appears on the inner pages of Attestations. In all probability, then, they are the Marines' own copies of their Continuous Service Certificates, written on more durable paper than that used for Attestations, and have found their way back into official custody. The references are ADM 157/2304-2470.

Attestations held in War Office Archives

There are some Royal Marine Attestations in WO 97/2170. The reason is no longer known, but they could be those of Royal Marines transferring to the Army.

8.5.3 Description Books (ADM 158)

The surviving Description Books comprise the record class ADM 158, and cover in general the years 1755 to 1940. They are arranged by Division and then by Company within the Division. They were drawn up using the information provided on the Attestations; and hence will contain information paralleling surviving Attestations but fill gaps where the Attestation is no longer extant. They consist of several different though related types of register, arranged by date of Attestation under the initial letter of the Marine's surname. Strict alphabetical order was not respected. The earliest Description Books, however, are arranged by Company number, the names being listed in no discernible order. Description Books state date of attestation (that is to say, of enlistment), age at attestation, place of attestation, parish of birth, previous occupation, a brief physical description and an indication of promotions or casualties. By the last is meant an indication of the Royal Marine's discharge, or date of death, or even desertion.

The arrangements by Division and date are as follows. **Miscellaneous** Description Books, 1755 to 1803, give an haphazard coverage; only Chatham Division appears fairly well documented (ADM 158/1-6). There follow the Description Books of **Chatham Division**, 1790 to 1884 (ADM 158/7-32), **Woolwich Division**, 1796 (sic) to 1884 (ADM 158/33-90), **Royal Marine Artillery**, 1705 to 1884 (ADM 158/75, 77-90, 101, 108, 114, 124, 129, 137, 155, 161, 167, 171, 176, 182, 188, 194, 200-205), **Portsmouth Division**, 1796 to 1889 (ADM 158/91-206), **Plymouth Division**, uneven coverage 1763 to 1884 (ADM 158/207-283), and **Deal Depot**, 1881 to 1940 (ADM 158/284-299).

8.5.4 Records of Service (ADM 159)

A register of the surviving Service Records is in ADM 313/27-109. It is arranged by Division and date, then in alphabetical order. It provides the Marine's service number. Armed with all that information, you are ready to locate the service record.

Records of Service were officially introduced in December 1884, when a system of Divisional Numbers was introduced, giving each man his own distinctive number within his Division. The numbering was made retrospective to encompass the unofficial use of the numbering system, which, in some instances, anticipated regulations by upward of forty years.

Portsmouth Division, 1843 to 1901 (ADM 159/1-19); 1901 to 1925 (ADM 159/181-202); Short Service, 1914 to 1918 (ADM 159/203-208).

Royal Marine Artillery, 1859 to 1901 (ADM 159/20-35); 1901 to 1923 (ADM 159/80-94); Short Service, 1914 to 1920 (ADM 159/95-102).

Chatham Division, 1842 to 1905 (ADM 159/36-60); 1905 to [1935] (ADM 159/124-142 and 213); Short Service, 1914 to 1920 (ADM 159/143-149).

Plymouth Division, 1856 to 1902 (ADM 159/61-79); 1902 to 1936 (ADM 159/150-174); Short Service, 1914 to 1918 (ADM 159/175-180).

Woolwich Division was disbanded in 1869. Records of men who formerly served in the Woolwich Division, and who were still serving elsewhere in 1884 (when the Records of Service were officially introduced) will be found amongst the records of the Division into which the men were transferred.

Deal Depot, 1866 to 1925 (ADM 159/113-118); **Royal Marine Divisional Engineers**, Short Service, 1914 to 1916 (ADM 159/119-121); **Royal Marine Labour Corps**, 1919 (ADM 159/122 and 123).

In addition, for the First World War period, service records include those of the Royal Marines Band, Medical Unit, Depot, Divisional Train, Ordnance Company.

Entries are only very approximately in order of date of enlistment; and so, a search of record class ADM 159, without knowledge of the Royal Marine's service number, may be lengthy. A successful search should provide a wealth of information about the date and place of birth, trade, religion, date and place of enlistment, physical description, a full record of service with comments on conduct, promotions, award, medal entitlements, names of HM ships and shore stations served on **[Fig 4]**. The Service Records are subject to a seventy-five year closure period. References to Service Records will be included in the consolidated, nominal list that the Reader Services Department is preparing.

For information about Royal Marines who enlisted within the last seventy-five years, enquiries should be directed to:

Drafting and Record Office, Royal Marines
HMS *Centurion*
Grange Road
GOSPORT
Hampshire
PO13 9XA.

8.5.5 Effective and Subsistence Lists (ADM 96)

Effective and Subsistence Lists cover the period 1688 to 1837, and are to be found among the records of the Marine Pay Office. They contain no personal information, but have the advantage of listing men within Companies for each Division for purposes of pay and expenses. In some cases — for example, where a Marine is otherwise known to have served overseas for a time — they may well provide the information that will enable you to make a more informed search of other, more informative records.

8.5.6 HM Ships' Musters and Crew Lists (ADM 36 and ADM 37)

If the name of the HM ship upon which a Royal Marine served is known, together with the dates of that service, then the ships' musters and crew lists may be profitably consulted (ADM 36 and ADM 37). For information about a Marine in the years prior to the creation of the records mentioned in this section, HM ship's muster rolls are the only sources available to you. A word of warning, however: a speculative search has been known to take months before producing positive results[1]. The vessel's home and overseas stations can often be ascertained, too, from the annual *Navy List.* If prior to 1947, that information should enable you to determine the likely Division, as it was until then the policy for men of the home port Division to provide the ship's Royal Marine detachment.

8.5.7 Lady Marines

The stories concerning certain lady Marines can be authenticated in outline. A certain degree of adventitious ornament in the narratives must, of course, be expected. The most famous lady Marine was Hannah Snell, who went by the name of James Gray, and whose service dates are 1745 to 1750. The *Annual Register*, under the date 20 October 1761, carried an unverifiable statement by one Hannah Witney to the effect that she had been a Marine for about five years. Another lady Marine went under the name of Arthur Douglas, and served briefly on the privateer *Resolution*, commanded by Captain Barber (a 'Liverpool record' of 20 May 1757, not otherwise identified is my source of information). James Mace was the *nom de guerre* of yet another lady Marine, Jane Mace, whose story is told in *Lloyd's Evening Post and British Chronicles*, dated 1 December 1762, under the date line 'Uttoxeter, Nov. 25'. It goes without saying that any search for records of other putative lady Marines is dependent for its success upon your knowledge of the lady's male pseudonym.

[1] See the account of one researcher's experience as told by M Gillen, *The Search for John Small, First Fleeter,* Sydney, Library of Australian History, 1985.

9. OTHER SERVICE RECORDS

9.1 Medals

Campaign Medals awarded to Royal Marine officers and men are recorded in the Royal Naval Medal Rolls (ADM 171). Those records are, as far as we can determine, complete up to the year 1920. They are arranged alphabetically, whether for officers or for other ranks. During the First World War, many Royal Marines received not only Royal Naval medals but Army gallantry medals as well (WO 329). Therefore the records of the latter should also be searched, using as a help the nominal index on microfiche that is available in the Romilly Room. Other records are more scattered. Records of Long Service and Good Conduct Medals and of the gratuities thereto attached, 1849 to 1894, are in ADM 201/21. As clause 85 of the Marine Mutiny Act required the churchwardens of the Royal Marine's parish to affix to the church door a statement to the effect that he had been awarded the Long Service and Good Conduct Medal, the Admiralty's Descriptive Return can sometimes be found among parish records[1]. Records concerning the qualifying service for the award of Campaign Stars, 1939 to 1945, are in ADM 201/110. Awards and decorations are gazetted in the *London Gazette*, which should be available in major research libraries, and of which a set is held by the PRO under the reference ZJ 1. In modern times, it is a monthly publication of considerable volume, containing, however, an index in every second volume. No original citations are known to be in the custody of the PRO, and none are believed to have survived at all from the First World War period, though occasionally a citation is reported in the *London Gazette*. Records concerning the award of foreign medals and decorations are to be found in the general registered files of the Foreign Office (FO 371). Recently the Ministry of Defence has deposited in the PRO scrap books containing extracts from publications naming winners of foreign medals (WO 379).

9.2 Courts Martial

The earliest records of Courts Martial of Royal Marine officers, dating from the creation of the Regiments for Sea Service, are contained in the State Papers Domestic, Military Entry Books, in SP 44 (held at Chancery Lane), and fully described elsewhere in this guide. Some of the volumes are indexed, others annotated in the margin of each page. The index or annotation takes the form simply of stating 'Court Martial' on such and such a page, or 'Warrant for a Court Martial'; sometimes the indication is a reference to a Judge Advocate. Those records do not contain transcripts of evidence: where surviving, that must be obtained from elsewhere, either Army or Royal Navy courts martial records. A wider search among the State Papers Domestic could also prove fruitful: you should begin such a speculative search by using the indexes to each volume of the published Calendars of State Papers. The Calendars should be available in major research libraries; complete runs are held on open access shelves at both Kew and Chancery Lane.

Records of Courts Martial of Naval and Royal Marine officers and men in the eighteenth

[1] E.g. the Return concerning Sgt Thomas Butlet, RMA, dated 14 March 1865, is among the papers of the Parish Chest, Wroughton (Wiltshire Record Office 551/61). I owe this reference to the kindness of Mrs Jean Cole.

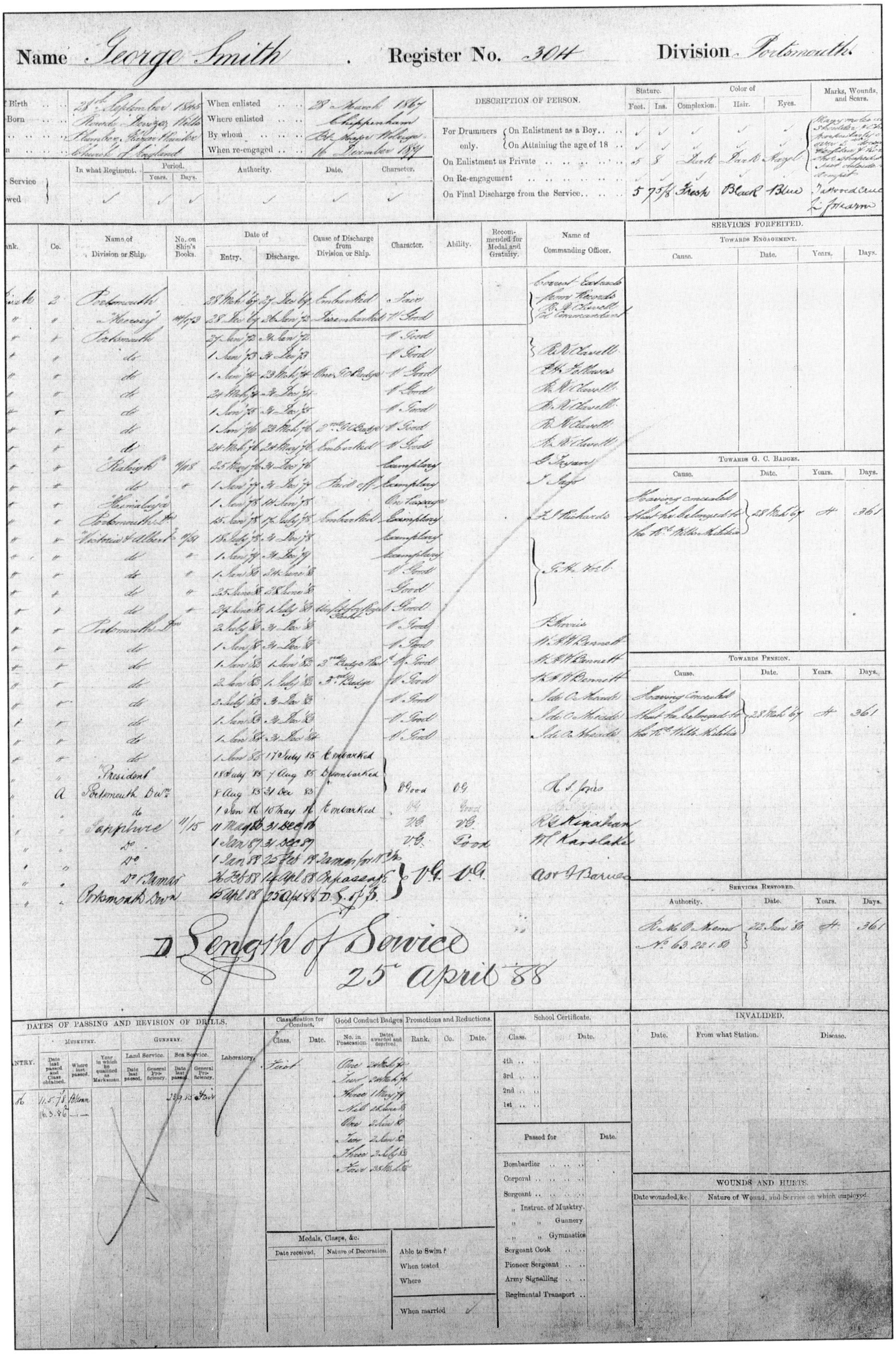

Name *George Smith*. Register No. *3014* Division *Portsmouth*

Birth	*28th September 1845*	When enlisted	*28 March 1867*
Born	*Rowde, Devizes, Wilts*	Where enlisted	*Chippenham*
		By whom	
	Church of England	When re-engaged	*16 December 1877*

DESCRIPTION OF PERSON.	Stature Feet	Ins.	Complexion	Hair	Eyes
On Enlistment as Private	5	8	*Dark*	*Dark*	*Hazel*
On Final Discharge from the Service	5	7 5/8	*Fresh*	*Black*	*Blue*

Length of Service 25th April 88

Figure 4 A typical Royal Marines other ranker's Service Record, ADM 159/1

and nineteenth centuries are to be found in record classes ADM 1 and ADM 194. Records in ADM 1 may be located through the various indexes and digests in ADM 12. For the years 1755 to 1806, alphabetical analyses and indexes to Courts Martial may be found in ADM 12/21-28. More detailed information about the surviving records of Courts Martial is given under the head: **Divisional Records**.

Records of Courts Martial held this century, covering the years 1911 to 1954, are in record class ADM 156. Not all are yet open to public inspection.

9.3 Obituary Books and Casualty Records

A short run of Obituary Books, recording the deaths of Royal Marine Officers (as well as Royal Navy officers) has survived for the middle years of the nineteenth century:

1833 to 1838 Obituary Book of Commissioned, Warrant and Marine Officers (ADM 11/51)

1839 to 1846 Ditto (ADM 11/52)

1846 to 1872 Ditto (ADM 6/448).

The Register of Reports of Deaths in Ships, for the years 1893 to 1909, is in ADM 104/109; the subsequent Registers of Reports of Deaths in Ships, covering the year 1910 to 1956, are in ADM 104/110-121 (ADM 104/120 and 121 are indexed), but closed to public inspection for a period of seventy-five years to date from the last entry in each. The indexes to those Registers, covering the years 1893 to 1950, are, however, open to public inspection (ADM 104/102-108).

ADM 242/7-10 constitute a war graves roll of the **First World War**, arranged alphabetically by surname of the dead Marine. Information provided there includes full Christian names, rank, service number, ship's name, date and place of birth, cause of death, where buried (precise plot number) and name of next of kin. Lists of Royal Marine officers and other rankers who died in the early years of the First World War are given in the annual *Navy Lists*, together with similar lists of Royal Naval officers and ratings. Indexes to the Registers of Killed and Wounded, 1915 to 1929, are in ADM 104/140-143. The Registers of Killed and Wounded, 1854 to 1911, and August 1914 to 1929, are in ADM 104/144 -149, and are indexed.

For the **Second World War** period, not all original records have yet been made publicly accessible by the Ministry of Defence. Nevertheless, you are not left without help, for on open access shelves in the Reference Room is an invaluable four volume publication, produced by the Royal Marines Museum, in 1987, entitled *A Register of Royal Marines' War Deaths, 1939-1945*. As well as providing a nominal roll of all Royal Marines who died in the Second World War, the volumes list them by ship and unit, and also provide burial details. The alphabetical Registers of Reports of Deaths of Naval Ratings of the Second World War period (September 1939 to June 1948), in ADM 104/127-139, contain information about Royal Marines as well as about Royal Naval ratings. They provide information concerning place of origin and cause of death; codes concerning the latter are apparently those used in the First World War registers (eg ADM 242/10).

9.4 Hospital Records

Hospital Musters for men of the Royal Navy and the Marines, 1740 to 1860, are in record class ADM 102.

A selection of hospital admission and discharge registers, 2nd General Hospital, for Royal Marines, 1918, is to be found in MH 106/986-997.

Making speculative searches may also be contemplated, focused on the war diaries of army aid posts and hospitals. They are included among the war diaries of the First World War in WO 95, for the Second World War in WO 169[1]. Surviving medical records can be difficult to locate, and certainly only a small percentage has been selected for permanent preservation. Help can be offered to you through a joint work of the Wellcome Medical Research Institute and the Public Record Office, whereby a data bank has been assembled, indicating the whereabouts and the extent of surviving records. Requests made to the PRO for such information will take a couple of days to process.

9.5 Prisoners of War

A nominal list of all Royal Marines known to have been held captive in German POW camps between 1939 and 1945 is to be found in ADM 201/111. Records concerning the repatriation of POWs from Korea, and covering such matters as the arrangements for their return and future employment, together with casualty information (ADM 201/109), have been retained by the Ministry of Defence, under section 3(4) of the Public Records Act 1958, as amended.

9.6 Coastguard Service of Royal Marines

Alphabetically arranged service record cards of Royal Marine other ranks and Royal Naval ratings who, between 1900 and 1923, undertook duty as coastguards, are in ADM 175/82A, 82B, 83B, 84A and 84B; of Royal Marines alone, 1919 to 1923, in ADM 175/90. The only way of distinguishing between the two types of servicemen is by observing the use of military rank for the Royal Marines, naval rank for the Royal Naval ratings.

9.7 Royal Marine Census, 1922

The returns of the census of Royal Marines, held on 28 February 1922, are in ADM 201/65.

9.8 Mobilization Returns and Complements of HM Ships

Mobilization Returns listing complements of HM ships, 1887 to 1939, are in ADM 286. They provide statistical information about officers and other ranks of the Royal Marines, together with similar information about the Royal Navy and the Fleet Air Arm. Whereas

---

[1] Army War Diaries of the Second World War period are closed to public inspection for a period of 100 years. However, the Ministry of Defence is willing to waive that restriction for researchers willing to sign an Undertaking of Confidentiality.

The Undertaking forms are available in the Reference Room.

earlier Returns had listed the complements of ships in Home Waters only, these records provide information about all HM ships and stations. However, they contain no personal information. They were prepared by the Mobilization Branch of the Admiralty, and published quarterly.

There is a gap in records of that type from 1939 until 1952, when begin the Complements of Ships prepared by the Director General of Naval Manpower, 1953 to 1968 (record class ADM 299). There are, too, some similar files in ADM 1. They provide statistical information about officers and men of Royal Marines Brigades and Depots. Researchers are reminded that certain files are still closed to public inspection for a period of thirty years to date from the latest entry each contains.

9.9 Ecclesiastical, Civil and Census Records

Ecclesiastical and civil registers should contain personal information about a Marine's birth, marriage and death. He should be entered upon the decennial population censuses if at home, in barracks or on board an HM ship in Home Waters. It is, however, quite usual to find in those instances that, while the officers have been named, only statistics of other rankers have been furnished. Finally, the Militia Ballot Lists, instituted in 1756, while not providing very detailed information, will nevertheless indicate whether a man was a Marine. Those records are not in the custody of the PRO and their survival has been most irregular.

9.10 Desertion

Records of desertions are to be found in the muster rolls and crew lists of HM ships (notably in record classes ADM 36 and ADM 37), where the siglum 'R' following a (Royal) Marine's name indicates that the man has 'run', that is to say, deserted.

Desertions of 1685 were recorded in the *London Gazette*, 5-8 January 1684/5, and 9-13 April 1685 (PRO reference ZJ 1/11).

The arrival of the Prince of Orange, in 1689, appears to have been the signal for mass desertions: 15,000 out of 30,000 men from the late King's army. Units, whose allegiance was in doubt, were transferred quickly to Holland or elsewhere abroad. The Royal Marines were disbanded on 28 February 1688/9 (Harl. MSS 7018; BL, Add MSS 9756; Treasury Records, King's Warrant Book, vol viii, f 399).

The desertions continued in considerable number from both Marine Regiments during the first half of 1690 (*London Gazette*, April to June 1690, in ZJ 1/13). In using the evidence provided by the *London Gazette*, we are putting to profit proclamations for the apprehension of deserters. It is likely that a wider ranging, though of course speculative, search through the pages of the *London Gazette*, would reveal information about numerous other desertions of Royal Marines.

Personal details of deserters are given in those proclamations, including information about their uniforms, which many researchers will find of interest.

Records of deserters from Chatham Division, 1842 to 1867, are in ADM 158/10.

Many cases of desertion were apparently technical, as sometimes it would simply have been a case of over-stayed leave or of a journey the duration of which had been miscalculated. The Marine's record was altered immediately on his reporting for duty. In the case of serious offenders, however, the matter very likely went to Court Martial; and so, records of Courts Martial may contain the wanted details of a desertion.

A Return of the Boer War period shows the number of Royal Marines entered, discharged and deserted, November 1899 to January 1900 (ADM 201/53).

9.11 Pension Records of Royal Marines

In general, pension records of Royal Marines and their families are similar to those of the Royal Navy (ADM 165 and ADM 166): the Royal Hospital at Greenwich was, in fact, founded to bring aid to the members of the Royal Navy and of the (Royal) Marines.

There are two alphabetical registers of **Royal Marine Officers** in receipt of Greenwich Hospital pensions, 1862 to 1908, which provide a considerable amount of personal and service information about the pensioners (ADM 201/22 and 23). Greenwich Hospital Warrants are in WO 23.

Records of Royal Marine officers' retired pay, 1871 to 1923, are in ADM 22/475-487. Researchers are referred, too, to records of officers on half pay.

9.12 Pensions awarded to Royal Marines' Families

Records of pensions paid to **widows of Royal Marine officers** will be found in ADM 96/523 (1712 to 1831), PMG 16 (1836 to 1870), PMG 20 (1870 to 1919) and PMG 72 (1921 to 1926). Other similar records, for the years 1880 to 1885, are in ADM 23/134, and for the years 1899 to 1932, in ADM 23/161. Similar records of pensions paid to the **widows of other rankers**, 1870 to 1919, are in PMG 72.

Records of pensions paid to **officers' children**, 1837 to 1931, are in PMG 18; those for **other rankers' children** are in ADM 166. Relevant with regard to minors, too, are the registers of Powers of Attorney, 1800 to 1899 (PMG 51).

9.13 Wills and Administrations

There is a collection of Marines' Wills and Letters of Administration, 1740 to 1764, in ADM 96/524. Wills were later deposited by Royal Marine other rankers in the Royal Navy Pay Office (ADM 48, indexed in ADM 142). There has survived, too, a register of probates affecting the payment of pensions, 1836 to 1915 (PMG 50).

10. RECORDS OF ROYAL MARINES' FAMILIES

10.1 Next of Kin

Wives and children of Royal Marines who followed their husbands and fell into financial distress appear to have been eligible for the Parish Relief. The Parish could apply to the wife's home parish for reimbursement. The records may have survived among parish records in local repositories[1].

Details of next of kin sometimes appear in Attestations. They appear, too, in the Registers of Killed and Wounded in the class of Royal Naval Medical Department records of the First World War period (ADM 104).

10.2 Registers of Births, Marriages and Deaths

Each Division maintained its own registers of births, marriages and deaths: thus recording the principal events of a Royal Marine's family life. The registers list, as well, the Marine's name and rank; and under the head 'disposal', some information on postings from the Division to ship or station.

Their survival has been haphazard, as the following table will show:

Chatham Division, 1830 to 1913, (ADM 183/114-120)

Plymouth Division, 1862 to 1920 (ADM 184/43-54)

Woolwich Division (marriage registers only), 1822 to 1869 (ADM 81/23-25)

Royal Marine Artillery, 1810 to 1853 (ADM 193/9), 1866 to 1921 (ADM 5/437)

Portsmouth Division (marriage registers only), 1869 to 1881 (ADM 185/69).

10.3 Widows and Children: Pensions, Wills and Administrations

See the section above on Pension Records and on Wills and Administrations.

10.4 Orphans of Royal Marines

Names of orphan children, whether boys or girls, of Royal Marines figure, with those of orphan children of Royal Naval personnel, among the Registers of Application for Entry to the Royal Naval Hospital, Greenwich, 1803 to 1930 (ADM 161), which are for the most part indexed. There are, too, indexed Registers of Claims for Maintenance of Orphan Daughters of Warrant Officers, Seamen and Marines, 1882 to 1925, in ADM 162/1, 2 and 9, together with indexed Registers of Claims for Admission of Orphan Boys to Orphanages at the Expense of Greenwich Hospital Funds, 1884 to 1959 (ADM 162/3-8). The series was discontinued in 1959.

[1] The Portsea Parish Vestry Clerk's record concerning Hannah Theurne and two daughters, wife of a Royal Marine embarked for a foreign station, has survived among the parish records of North Bradley (Wiltshire Record Office 533/50). I owe this information to the kindness of Mrs Jean Cole.

APPENDIX 1: TABLE SHOWING THE DISTRIBUTION OF COMPANIES THROUGHOUT THE DIVISIONS

Coy No	From 1757	1763	1777	1778	1779	1782	1783	1786	1789	1792	1795
1	PO	CH	CH	CH	CH	CH	CH	CH	CH	CH	CH
2	PL	PO	PO	PO	PO	PO	PO	PO	PO	PO	PO
3	CH	PL	PL	PL	PL	PL	PL	PL	PL	PL	PL
4	PO	CH	CH	CH	CH	CH	CH	CH	CH	CH	CH
5	PL	PO	PO	PO	PO	PO	PO	PO	PO	PO	PO
6	CH	PL	PL	PL	PL	PL	PL	PL	PL	PL	PL
7	PO	CH	CH	CH	CH	CH	CH	CH	CH	CH	CH
8	PL	PO	PO	PO	PO	PO	PO	PO	PO	PO	PO
9	CH	PL	PL	PL	PL	PL	PL	PL	PL	PL	PL
10	PO	CH	CH	CH	CH	CH	CH	CH	CH	CH	CH
11	PL	PO	PO	PO	PO	PO	PO	PO	PO	PO	PO
12	CH	PL	PL	PL	PL	PL	PL	PL	PL	PL	PL
13	PO	CH	CH	CH	CH	CH	CH	CH	CH	CH	CH
14	PL	PO	PO	PO	PO	PO	PO	PO	PO	PO	PO
15	CH	PL	PL	PL	PL	PL	PL	PL	PL	PL	PL
16	PO	CH	CH	CH	CH	CH	CH	CH	CH	CH	CH
17	PL	PO	PO	PO	PO	PO	PO	PO	PO	PO	PO
18	CH	PL	PL	PL	PL	PL	PL	PL	PL	PL	PL
19	PO	CH	CH	CH	CH	CH	CH	CH	CH	CH	CH
20	PL	PO	PO	PO	PO	PO	PO	PO	PO	PO	PO
21	CH	PL	PL	PL	PL	PL	PL	PL	PL	PL	PL
22	PO	CH	CH	CH	CH	CH	CH	CH	CH	CH	CH
23	PL	PO	PO	PO	PO	PO	PO	PO	PO	PO	PO
24	CH	PL	PL	PL	PL	PL	PL	PL	PL	PL	PL
25	PO	CH	CH	CH	CH	CH	CH	CH	CH	CH	CH
26	PL	PO	PO	PO	PO	PO	PO	PO	PO	PO	PO
27	CH	PL	PL	PL	PL	PL	PL	PL	PL	PL	PL
28	PO	CH	CH	CH	CH	CH	CH	CH	CH	CH	CH
29	PL	PO	PO	PO	PO	PO	PO	PO	PO	PO	PO
30	CH	PL	PL	PL	PL	PL	PL	PL	PL	PL	PL
31	PO	CH	CH	CH	CH	CH	CH	CH	CH	CH	CH
32	PL	PO	PO	PO	PO	PO	PO	PO	PO	PO	PO
33	CH	PL	PL	PL	PL	PL	PL	PL	PL	PL	PL
34	PO	CH	CH	CH	CH	CH	CH	CH	CH	CH	CH
35	PL	PO	PO	PO	PO	PO	PO	PO	PO	PO	PO
36	CH	PL	PL	PL	PL	PL	PL	PL	PL	PL	PL
37	PO	CH	CH	CH	CH	CH	CH	CH	CH	CH	CH
38	PL	PO	PO	PO	PO	PO	PO	PO	PO	PO	PO
39	PO	PL	PL	PL	PL	PL	PL	PL	PL	PL	PL

Coy No	From 1799	1800	1801	1802	1805	1806
1	CH	CH	CH	CH	CH	CH
2	PO	PO	PO	PO	PO	PO
3	PL	PL	PL	PL	PL	PL
4	CH	CH	CH	CH	CH	CH
5	PO	PO	PO	PO	PO	PO
6	PL	PL	PL	PL	PL	PL
7	CH	CH	CH	CH	CH	CH
8	PO	PO	PO	PO	PO	PO
9	PL	PL	PL	PL	PL	PL
10	CH	CH	CH	CH	CH	CH
11	PO	PO	PO	PO	PO	PO
12	PL	PL	PL	PL	PL	PL
13	CH	CH	CH	CH	CH	CH
14	PO	PO	PO	PO	PO	PO
15	PL	PL	PL	PL	PL	PL
16	CH	CH	CH	CH	CH	CH
17	PO	PO	PO	PO	PO	PO
18	PL	PL	PL	PL	PL	PL
19	CH	CH	CH	CH	CH	CH
20	PO	PO	PO	PO	PO	PO
21	CH	CH	CH	CH	CH	CH
22	PO	PO	PO	PO	PO	PO
23	PL	PL	PL	PL	PL	PL
24	CH	CH	CH	CH	CH	CH
25	PO	PO	PO	PO	PO	PO
26	PL	PL	PL	PL	PL	PL
27	CH	CH	CH	CH	CH	CH
28	PO	PO	PO	PO	PO	PO
29	PL	PL	PL	PL	PL	PL
30	CH	CH	CH	CH	CH	CH
31	PO	PO	PO	PO	PO	PO
32	PL	PL	PL	PL	PL	PL
33	CH	CH	CH	CH	CH	CH
34	PO	PO	PO	PO	PO	PO
35	PL	PL	PL	PL	PL	PL
36	CH	CH	CH	CH	CH	CH
37	PO	PO	PO	PO	PO	PO
38	PL	PL	PL	PL	PL	PL
39	CH	CH	CH	CH	CH	CH

Coy No	From 1815	1817	1838	1850	1869
1	CH	CH	CH	CH	CH
2	PO	PO	PO	PO	PO
3	PL	PL	PL	PL	PL
4	WO	WO	WO	WO	CH
5	CH	CH	CH	CH	CH
6	PO	PO	PO	PO	PO
7	PL	PL	PL	PL	PL
8	WO	WO	WO	WO	PO
9	CH	CH	CH	CH	CH
10	PO	PO	PO	PO	PO
11	PL	PL	PL	PL	PL
12	WO	WO	WO	WO	PL
13	CH	CH	CH	CH	CH
14	PO	PO	PO	PO	PO
15	PL	PL	PL	PL	PL
16	WO	WO	WO	WO	CH
17	CH	CH	CH	CH	CH
18	PO	PO	PO	PO	PO
19	PL	PL	PL	PL	PL
20	WO	WO	WO	WO	PO
21	CH	CH	CH	CH	CH
22	PO	PO	PO	PO	PO
23	PL	PL	PL	PL	PL
24	WO	WO	WO	WO	PL
25	CH	CH	CH	CH	CH
26	PO	PO	PO	PO	PO
27	PL	PL	PL	PL	PL
28	WO	WO	WO	WO	CH
29	CH	CH	CH	CH	CH
30	PO	PO	PO	PO	PO
31	PL	PL	PL	PL	PL
32	WO	WO	WO	WO	PO
33	CH	CH	CH	CH	CH
34	PO	PO	PO	PO	PO
35	PL	PL	PL	PL	PL
36	WO	WO	WO	WO	PL
37	CH	CH	CH	CH	CH
38	PO	PO	PO	PO	PO
39	PL	PL	PL	PL	PL

40	PL	CH	CH	CH	CH	CH	CH	CH	CH	CH	CH
41	PO	PO	PO	PO	PO	PO	PO	PO	PO	PO	PO
42	PL	PL	PL	PL	PL	PL	PL	PL	PL	PL	PL
43	PO	CH	CH	CH	CH	CH	CH	CH	CH	CH	CH
44	PL	PO	PO	PO	PO	PO	PO	PO	PO	PO	PO
45	PO	PL	PL	PL	PL	PL	PL	PL	PL	PL	PL
46	PL	CH	CH	CH	CH	CH	CH	CH	CH	CH	CH
47	PO	PO	PO	PO	PO	PO	PO	PO	PO	PO	PO
48	PL	PL	PL	PL	PL	PL	PL	PL	PL	PL	PL
49	PO	PO	PO	PO	PO	PO	CH	CH	CH	CH	CH
50	PO	PL	PL	PL	PL	PL	PO	PO	PO	PO	PO
51	PO	PO	PO	PO	PO	PO	PL	PL	PL	PL	PL
52	PL	PL	PL	PL	PL	PL	CH	CH	CH	CH	CH
53	CH	PO	PO	PO	PO	PO	PO	PO	PO	PO	PO
54	PO	PL	PL	PL	PL	PL	PL	PL	PL	PL	PL
55	PL	PO	PO	PO	PO	PO	CH	PO	PO	PO	PO
56	CH	PL	PL	PL	PL	PL	PO	PL	PO	PO	PO
57	PO	PO	PO	PO	PO	PO	PL	PO	PL	PL	PL
58	PL	PL	PL	PL	PL	PL	CH	PL	PL	PL	PL
59	CH	PO	PO	PO	PO	PO	PO	PO	PO	PO	PO
60	PO	PL	PL	PL	PL	PL	PL	PL	PL	PL	PL
61	PL	PO	PO	PO	PO	PO	PO	PO	PO	PO	PO
62	CH	PL	PL	PL	PL	PL	PL	PL	PL	PL	PL
63	PO	PO	PO	PO	PO	PO	PO	PO	PO	PO	PO
64	PL	PL	PL	PL	PL	PL	PL	PL	PL	PL	PL
65	CH	PO	PO	PO	PO	PO	PO		CH	CH	CH
66	PO	PL	PL	PL	PL	PL	PL		PO	PO	PO
67	PL	PO	PO	PO	PO	PO	PO		PL	PL	PL
68	CH	PL	PL	PL	PL	PL	PL		CH	CH	CH
69	PO	PO	PO	PO	PO	PO	PO		PO	PO	PO
70	PL	PL	PL	PL	PL	PL	PL		PL	PL	PL
71	CH		CH	CH	CH	CH				CH	CH
72	PO		PO	PO	PO	PO				PO	PO
73	PL		PL	PL	PL	PL				PL	PL
74	CH		CH	CH	CH	CH				CH	CH
75	PO		PO	PO	PO	PO				PO	PO
76	PL		PL	PL	PL	PL				PL	PL
77	CH		CH	CH	CH	CH				CH	CH
78	PO		PO	PO	PO	PO				PO	PO
79	PL		PL	PL	PL	PL				PL	PL
80	CH		PO	PO	PO	PO				CH	CH
81	PO		PL	PL	PL	PL				PO	PO
82	PL		PO	PO	PO	PO				PL	PL
83	CH		PL	PL	PL	PL				CH	CH
84	PO		PO	PO	PO	PO				PO	PO
85	PL		PL	PL	PL	PL				PL	PL
86	CH			CH	CH	CH				CH	CH
87	PO			PO	PO	PO				PO	PO
88	PL			PL	PL	PL				PL	PL
89	CH			CH	CH	CH				CH	CH
90	PO			PO	PO	PO				PO	PO

40	PO	PO	PO	PO	PO	PO
41	PO	PO	PO	PO	PO	PO
42	PL	PL	PL	PL	PL	PL
43	CH	CH	CH	CH	CH	CH
44	CH	PO	PO	PO	PO	PO
45	PL	PL	PL	PL	PL	PL
46	CH	CH	CH	CH	CH	CH
47	PO	PO	PO	PO	PO	PO
48	PL	PL	PL	PL	PL	PL
49	CH	CH	CH	CH	CH	CH
50	PO	PO	PO	PO	PO	PO
51	PL	PL	PL	PL	PL	PL
52	CH	CH	CH	CH	CH	CH
53	PO	PO	PO	PO	PO	PO
54	PL	PL	PL	PL	PL	PL
55	PO	PO	CH	CH	CH	CH
56	PO	PO	PO	PO	PO	PO
57	PL	PL	PL	PL	PL	PL
58	PL	PL	CH	CH	CH	CH
59	PO	PO	PO	PO	PO	PO
60	PL	PL	PL	PL	PL	PL
61	PO	PO	CH	CH	CH	CH
62	PL	PO	PO	PO	PO	PO
63	PO	PO	PL	PL	PL	PL
64	PL	PL	CH	CH	CH	CH
65	CH	CH	PO	PO	PO	PO
66	PO	PO	PL	PL	PL	PL
67	PL	PL	CH	CH	CH	CH
68	CH	CH	PO	PO	PO	PO
69	PO	PO	PL	PL	PL	PL
70	PL	PL	CH	CH	CH	CH
71	CH	CH	PO	PO	PO	PO
72	PO	PO	PL	PL	PL	PL
73	PL	PL	CH	CH	CH	CH
74	CH	CH	PO	PO	PO	PO
75	PO	PO	PL	PL	PL	PL
76	PL	PL	CH	CH	CH	CH
77	CH	CH	PO	PO	PO	PO
78	PO	PO	PL	PL	PL	PL
79	PL	PL	CH	CH	CH	CH
80	CH	CH	PO	PO	PO	PO
81	PO	PO	PL	PL	PL	PL
82	PL	PL	CH	CH	CH	CH
83	CH	CH	PO	PO	PO	PO
84	PO	PO	PL	PL	PL	PL
85	PL	PL	CH	CH	CH	CH
86	CH	CH	PO	PO	PO	PO
87	PO	PO	PL	PL	PL	PL
88	PL	PL	CH	CH	CH	CH
89	CH	CH	PO	PO	PO	PO
90	PO	PO	PL	PL	PL	PL

40	WO	WO	WO	WO	CH
41	CH	CH	CH	CH	CH
42	PO	PO	PO	PO	PO
43	PL	PL	PL	PL	PL
44	WO	WO	WO	WO	PO
45	CH	CH	CH	CH	CH
46	PO	PO	PO	PO	PO
47	PL	PL	PL	PL	PL
48	WO	WO	WO	WO	PL
49	CH	CH	CH	CH	CH
50	PO	PO	PO	PO	PO
51	PL	PL	PL	PL	PL
52	WO	WO	WO	WO	CH
53	CH	CH	CH	CH	CH
54	PO	PO	PO	PO	PO
55	PL	PL	PL	PL	PL
56	WO	CH	CH	WO	PO
57	CH	PO	PO	CH	CH
58	PO	PL	PL	PO	PO
59	PL	CH	CH	PL	PL
60	WO	PO	PO	WO	PL
61	CH	PL	PL	CH	CH
62	PO	CH	CH	CH	PO
63	PL	PO	PO	PL	PL
64	WO	PL	PL	WO	CH
65	CH	CH	CH	CH	CH
66	PO	PO	PO	PO	PO
67	PL	PL	PL	PL	PL
68	WO	PO	PO	WO	PL
69	CH	PL	PL	CH	CH
70	PO	CH	CH	PO	PO
71	PL	PL	PL	PL	PL
72	WO	CH	CH	WO	PL
73	CH	CH	CH	CH	CH
74	PO	PO	PO	PO	PO
75	PL	PL	PL	PL	PL
76	WO	WO	WO	WO	CH
77	CH	CH	CH	CH	CH
78	PO	PO	PO	PO	PO
79	PL	PL	PL	PL	PL
80	WO	WO	WO	WO	PO
81	CH	CH	CH	CH	CH
82	PO	PO	PO	PO	PO
83	PL	PL	PL	PL	PL
84	WO	CH	WO	WO	PL
85	CH	PO	PO	CH	
86	PO	PO	PO	PO	
87	PL	PO	PO	PL	
88	WO	PL	WO	WO	
89	CH	WO	WO	CH	
90	PO	PO	PO	PO	

140	PL
141	PO
142	PL
143	PO
144	PL
145	PO
146	PL
147	CH
148	PO
149	PL
150	PO
151	PL

142	CH	PO	PO	PO
143	CH	PL	PL	PL
144	PO		WO	WO
145	PL		WO	WO
146			WO	WO
147			WO	WO
148			WO	WO
149			WO	WO
150			WO	WO
151			WO	WO
152			WO	WO
153			WO	WO
154			WO	WO
155			WO	WO
156			WO	WO
157			WO	WO
158			WO	WO
159			WO	WO
160			WO	WO
161			WO	WO
162			WO	WO
163			WO	WO
164			WO	WO
165			WO	WO
166			WO	WO
167			WO	WO
168			WO	WO
169			WO	WO
170			WO	WO
171			WO	WO
172			WO	WO
173			WO	WO
174				WO
175				WO
176				WO
177				WO
178				WO
179				WO
180				WO
181				WO
182				WO
183				WO

91	PL	PL	PL	PL	PL	PL
92	CH	CH	CH	CH	CH	CH
93	PO	PO	PO	PO	PO	PO
94	CH	PL	PL	PL	PL	PL
95	PL	CH	CH	CH	CH	CH
96	CH	CH	CH	CH	PO	PO
97	CH	CH	CH	CH	PL	PL
98	CH	CH	CH	CH	CH	CH
99	CH	CH	CH	CH	PO	PO
100	CH	CH	CH	CH	PL	PL
101	PO	PO	PO	PO		CH
102	PL	PL	PL	PL		PO
103	CH	PO	PO	PO		PL
104	PO	PL	PL	PL		CH
105	PL	PO	PO	PO		PO
106	CH	PL	PL	PL		PL
107	PO	PO	PO	PO		CH
108	PL	PL	PL	PL		PO
109	CH	PO	PO	PO		PL
110	PO	PL	PL	PL		CH
111	PL	CH	CH	CH		PO
112	CH	PO	PO	PO		PL
113	PO	PL	PL	PL		CH
114	PL	CH	CH	CH		PO
115	CH	PO	PO	PO		PL
116	PO	PL	PL	PL		CH
117	PL	CH	CH	CH		PO
118	CH	PO	PO	PO		PL
119	PO	PL	PL	PL		CH
120	PL	CH	CH	CH		PO
121	CH	PO	PO	PO		PL
122	PO	PL	PL	PL		
123	PL	CH	CH	CH		
124	CH	PO	PO	PO		
125	PO	PL	PL	PL		
126	PL		PO	PO		
127	CH		PL	PL		
128	PO		PO	PO		
129	PL		PL	PL		
130	CH		PO	PO		
131			PL	PL		
132			PO	PO		
133			PL	PL		
134			PO	PO		
135			PL	PL		
134				PO		
135				PL		
136				CH		
137				PO		
138				PL		
139				PO		

91	PL	PL	CH	CH	CH	CH
92	CH	CH	PO	PO	PO	PO
93	PO	PO	PL	PL	PL	PL
94	PL	PL	CH	CH	CH	CH
95	CH	CH	PO	PO	PO	PO
96	PO	PO	PL	PL	PL	PL
97	PL	PL	CH	CH	CH	CH
98	CH	CH	CH	CH	CH	CH
99	PO	PO	CH	CH	CH	CH
100	PL	PL	CH	CH	CH	CH
101	CH	CH		PO	PO	PO
102	PO	PO		PL	PL	PL
103	PL	PL		CH	CH	CH
104	CH	CH		PO	PO	PO
105	PO	PO		PL	PL	PL
106	PL	PL		CH	CH	CH
107	CH	CH		PO	PO	PO
108	PO	PO		PL	PL	PL
109	PL	PL		CH	CH	CH
110	CH	CH		PO	PO	PO
111	PO	PO		PL	PL	PL
112	PL	PL		CH	CH	CH
113	CH	CH		PO	PO	PO
114	PO	PO		PL	PL	PL
115	PL	PL		CH	CH	CH
116	CH	CH		PO	PO	PO
117	PO	PO		PL	PL	PL
118	PL	PL		CH	CH	CH
119	CH	CH		PO	PO	PO
120	PO	PO		PL	PL	PL
121	PL	PL		CH	CH	CH
122	CH	CH		PO	PO	PO
123	PO	PO		PL	PL	PL
124	PL	PL		CH	CH	CH
125	CH	CH		PO	PO	PO
126	PO	PO		PL	PL	PL
127	PL	PL		CH	CH	CH
128	CH	CH		PO	PO	PO
129	PO	PO		PL	PL	PL
130	PL	PL		CH	CH	CH
131	PO	PO		PO	PO	PO
132	PL	PL		PL	PL	PL
133	PO	PO		CH	CH	CH
134	PL	PL		PO	PO	PO
135	PO	PO		PL	PL	PL
136	PL	PL		PO	PO	PO
137	PO	PO		PL	PL	PL
138	PL	PL		PO	PO	PO
139	PO	PO		PL	PL	PL
140	PL	PL		PO	PO	PO
141		CH		PL	PL	PL

91	PL	PL	CH	PL
92	WO	PO	PO	WO
93	CH	PL	PL	CH
94	PO	WO	WO	PO
95	PL	CH	CH	PL
96	WO	PO	WO	WO
97	CH	PL	WO	CH
98	PO	WO	WO	PO
99	PL	CH	WO	PL
100	CH	PO	WO	WO
101	PO	PO	CH	PO
102	PL	PO	PO	PO
103	CH		PL	PL
104	PO		WO	PL
105	PL		CH	CH
106	CH		PO	CH
107	PO		PL	PO
108	PL		WO	PL
109	CH		CH	PL
110	PO		PO	PL
111	PL		PL	WO
112	CH		WO	WO
113	PL			CH
114	CH			PO
115	PL			PL
116	CH			WO
117	CH			
118	CH			
119	CH			
120	CH			

APPENDIX 2

HINTS ON IDENTIFYING A ROYAL MARINE'S DIVISION

Given the importance of the Divisional structure of the Royal Marines Corps, both in understanding its organization and functioning, and also in the service life of the individual Marine, you will need at times to identify a Royal Marine's Division. An unaided, speculative search will prove very time- consuming. For that reason, I have decided to suggest some means of making that search a little more structured.

1. Do you know his service number?

A Royal Marine's service number can often be found on personal effects or medals. It is often prefixed by the two letter abbreviation of his Division (CH, PO, PL).

2. Do you know the name of an HM ship he served on, and the date?

Consult the *Navy List* for the year and the ship's muster rolls to ascertain the ship's 'home' port. Prior to 1947, HM ships' Royal Marine detachments were drawn from the same RM Division as the 'home' port of the ship.

3. Do you know any of his medal entitlements?

Consult the rolls of Royal Marines who were recipients of the particular campaign or service medal.

4. Do you know his place of domicile and a date from the Census or from a Birth or Marriage Certificate?

He belonged in all likelihood to the immediately surrounding Divisional 'catchment area' (clear enough in general, but fuzzy at the edges).

5. Do you know his Company Number and a Date?

1. Consult the tables of allocation of Company Numbers to Divisions as set out in the *List of Officers of the Royal Marines* for the given year.

2. Consult the tables set out in Appendix 1.

6. Was he a war casualty?

Consult the nominal lists referred to under the head 'casualties'.

APPENDIX 3

SOME ADDRESSES OF OTHER RECORD REPOSITORIES

A. LOCAL AUTHORITY RECORD OFFICES

Reference has been made in this guide to the fact or the possibility that certain records have or may have been entrusted to the custody of county or other local record offices. Details of the holdings of each, and information about opening times and addresses, can be found in J Foster and J Sheppard, *British Archives: A Guide to Archival Resources in the United Kingdom*, 2nd edn, London, 1988. In briefer form, similar information is presented in *Record Repositories in Great Britain*, 9th edn, London, HMSO,1991.

B. NATIONAL RECORD OFFICES

B.1 Scottish Record Office

Some military records pertaining to Scottish units are held at the

Scottish Record Office
HM General Register House
EDINBURGH
EH1 3YY.

The SRO cannot undertake commissions of research for the public, but is accessible to researchers holding a valid reader's ticket.

B.2 Northern Ireland Record Office

Similar records pertaining to Northern Ireland since partition, 1921, are in the custody of the

Public Record Office of Northern Ireland
66 Balmoral Avenue
BELFAST
BT9 6NY,

which cannot undertake commissions of research for the public, but is accessible to readers holding a valid reader's ticket.

C. ROYAL MARINES, MILITARY AND NAVAL MUSEUMS

C.1 Royal Marines Museum and Library

The official museum and library of the Royal Marines has been established in the former Mess Building of the Royal Marines' Barracks at Eastney, itself a work of interesting military architecture. With particular responsibility for material records, written records of a non-official type (private papers, letters, diaries, mess books, uniforms, medals, panoramas of the Falklands War and Arctic warfare) together with a substantial library of printed works, it is located at the

Royal Marines Museum and Library
Royal Marines Barracks
EASTNEY
Hampshire
PO4 9PX,

where researchers are welcome after preliminary enquiry 01705-819 385.

C.2 Imperial War Museum
With a similar range of responsibilities, including custody of captured enemy records, but with holdings limited to records left by the wars of this century, together with a substantial library of printed works, is the

Imperial War Museum
Lambeth Road
LONDON
SE1 6HZ,

where researchers are welcome following preliminary enquiry 0171-735 8922.

C.3 National Army Museum
Having wider responsibility and holdings is the

National Army Museum
Royal Hospital Road
LONDON
SW3 4HT.

The museum mounts displays of material documents left by military engagements that have involved Great Britain. It possesses an important library of printed works, together with some copies of public records. Its fulcrum is, of course, the Army, but the degree to which the Royal Marines show similarities with the Army, and the growth of Combined Operations, mean that some records pertinent to the Royal Marines are included. It does not undertake commissions of research for the public, but is accessible to researchers in possession of a valid readers' ticket and following preliminary enquiry 0171-730 0717.

C.4 National Maritime Museum, Greenwich
Holding records, both private and public, concerning HM ships and their crews, together with an important library of published works, is the

National Maritime Museum
Romney Road
Greenwich
LONDON
SE10 9NF,

where researchers are welcome, following preliminary enquiry 0181-858 4422.

D. BRITISH LIBRARY

The British Library is one of the places of legal deposit for publications of the United Kingdom; which means that a copy of all published works should have been deposited there. The Library also has an Official Publications Department. The address at present is

The British Library
Great Russell Street
LONDON
WC1B 3DG
0171-323 7676

The British Library is open to *bona fide* researchers holding a valid reader's ticket. The same requirements hold for the

British Library
Newspaper Library
Colindale Avenue
LONDON
NW9 5HE
0171-323 7353

and for

British Library
Oriental and India Office Collections
Orbit House
197 Blackfriars Road
LONDON
SE1 8NG
0171-412 7873 & 0171-412 7000

E. OFFICE OF POPULATION CENSUSES AND SURVEYS

E.1 England and Wales

Records of the civil registration of births, marriages and deaths that have occurred in England and Wales since 1 July 1837 are in the custody of the

General Register Office
Office of Population Censuses and Surveys
St Catherine's House
10 Kingsway
LONDON
WC2B 6JP

where researchers **in person** have access to the lists and order copies of certificates.

Written applications, on the other hand, should be addressed to the

Postal Application Section
General Register Office
Office of Population Censuses and Surveys
Smedley Hydro
Trafalgar Road
Birkdale
SOUTHPORT
Merseyside
PR8 2HH.

E.2 Scotland

Similar records pertaining particularly to Scotland and Scottish military personnel are held at

General Register Office for Scotland
New Register House
EDINBURGH
EH1 3YT.

E.3 Northern Ireland

Records of the Civil registration of births, marriages and deaths that have occurred in Northern Ireland since partition (1921) are in the custody of

General Register Office, Northern Ireland
Oxford House
49-55 Chichester Street
BELFAST
BT1 4HL
01232-235 211.

E.4 Republic of Ireland

Similar records pertaining to all Ireland and, since 1920, to the Republic of Ireland (Eire) are held at the

General Register Office
Joyce House
8-11 Lombard Street
DUBLIN 2
Republic of Ireland.

F. Society of Genealogists

Help in tracing surviving records of Royal Marines may be obtained from the

Society of Genealogists
14 Charterhouse Buildings
Goswell Road
LONDON
EC1M 7BA
0171-251 8799.

G. RECORDS NOT YET PUBLICLY ACCESSIBLE

G.1 Drafting and Record Office Royal Marines

For advice about personal records not yet available to the public, the

Drafting and Record Office, Royal Marines
HMS *Centurion*
Grange Road
GOSPORT
Hampshire
PO13 9XA
01705-822 351

may be able to offer some guidance.

G.2 Ministry of Defence, Navy

For advice about records of Royal Marine serving officers, the

The Commandant General
Royal Marines
Ministry of Defence (Navy)
Whitehall
LONDON
SW1

may be able to offer some guidance.

BIBLIOGRAPHY

The following short list of works concerning the Royal Marines does not aim at comprehensiveness, rather at providing an indication of works that the author had easy access to, and which are available to the public, on request, from the PRO Library, at Kew. The PRO references are given in brackets.

Anon, *The Royal Marines. The Admiralty Account of their Achievements, 1939-1943*, London, His Majesty's Stationery Office, 1944 (MN.73).

Anon, *The Royal Marines*, (Pritkin 'Pride of Britain' Series), London, Pritkin, 1971.

R H Bruce-Lockhart, *The Marines were There*, London, Putnam, 1950.

H E Blumberg, *Britain's Sea Soldiers, 1914-1919*, Devonport, Swift and Co, 1927.

L Edye, *The Historical Records of the Royal Marines, Volume I: 1664-1701*, London, Harrison and Sons, 1893. (All that was published.) (MN.181)

C Field, *Britain's Sea Soldiers, 1664-1914. A History of the Royal Marines and their Predecessors in Action*, 2 vols, Liverpool, Lyceum Press, 1924. (MN.180)

E Fraser and L G Carr-Laughton, *Royal Marine Artillery*, 2 vols, London, Royal United Service Institution, 1930.

A C Hampshire, *The Royal Marines' Tercentenary, 1664-1964*, Glasgow, Paramount Press, 1964.

A J Lowe (editor), *Records of the Portsmouth Division of Marines, 1764-1800* (Portsmouth Record Series, 7), Portsmouth,1990.

A J Marini, 'Parliament and the Marine Regiments, 1739', *The Mariner's Mirror*, 62, 1976, pp 55-65 (BD.35).

J L Moulton, *The Royal Marines* ('Famous Regiments' Series), London, Leo Cooper, 1972 (MN.180).

P C Smith, *Per Mare, Per Terram*, St Ives, Photo Precision, 1972. (Not held by PRO)

The Globe and Laurel, the magazine of the Royal Marines, published by the Royal Marines Museum. Publication began 1st May, 1892; at present a bi-monthly publication. (Not held by PRO)

INDEX

This index has been been drawn up to supplement the Table of Contents. It is not intended to be exhaustive and is limited to referring to specific matters that the more general titles of the Table of Contents might miss.

A

Admiralty Leave Books 39
Amphibian Support Regiment 32
Amphibious School 32
Artillery
    Royal 3
    Royal Marine 3
    Marine, Companies of 3
Ashanti 20

B

Bands
    Commandant General Royal Marines Squad 36
    Leech-Porter Committee 36
    'Redeployment Plan' 36
    Royal Marines Band Service 36
Baptisms, Sheerness Royal Marines' Church 18, 54
Barracks
    Forton 3
    Gosport 3, 15
    Portsmouth 3, 15
Births, Marriages and Deaths, Registers 54

C

Candlestick, King's 34
Canton 19
Chapel of the Royal Naval College 34
China 10, 17. 19
Circulars and General Instructions 26
Clothing 6, 7
Colours, presentation of 34
Combined Operations 26, 30, 31,34, 40
    Lists of Combined Operations Royal Naval and Royal Marine Officers 40
Companies 3
Commandant General's Office
    Royal Marine Office 4
Commissions and Appointments Registers 37
Continuous Service Certificates 5, 19
Corporal Tom Hunter, VC, RM, Memorial Cottages 34
Correspondence 4

D

Depot, Reserve, Exmouth 27
Director General, Naval Manpower 29, 52
Discharge by Purchase 19
Division 3, 9, 42
Divisional Despatches 27
Dress Regulations 7

E

Embarkation Books 39
Esquimault 20
Establishment Lists 37
Exmouth Reserve Depot 27

F

Fleet
    British Pacific 27
    Home 27
    Mediterranean 27

G

Globe and Laurel 29, 39

H

Half Pay and Allowances 23, 40
Hospital Records 35, 51

I

Instructions, Rules and, 4, 5
Ireland 19

J

Japan 20
Joint Services 31

K

King's Candlestick 34

Korea 29, 51

L

Letters, Monthly 27
Loyal Toast 34

M

Marine Companies of Artillery 3
Marine Officers' List 6, 37
Marine Pay Office 1, 4
Mediterranean 19, 33
Mobile Naval Base Defence Organization 27
Monthly Letters 27

N

Naval Carrier Task Forces 32

O

Orders
  General and Instructions 5, 26
  Routine 26

P

Pay Office, (Royal) Marine 1, 4
Paymaster 4, 23
Paymasters' Agents 23
Prisoners of War, Royal Marines 51

R

Reorganization 30
Reports
  Special 27
  Weekly 27
Regulations
  Dress 7
  Sea 4, 5
  Shore 4, 5
Royal Artillery 3
Royal Marine Office *now* Commandant General's Office 4
Royal Marines Officers' List 6, 37
Royal Marines Pay Office 1, 4
Royal Marine Division, Second World War 27
Royal Marines Units
  Admiral's Regiment 1
  Duke of York and Albany's Maritime Regiment of Foot 1
  Prince George of Denmark's Maritime Regiment of Foot 1
  Six Marine Regiments 1
  Ten Marine Regiments 6
  (Royal Marines) Commandos 30-31
    Formation 30
    Organization 30-31
    Training 30-31
    No 3 Commando Brigade 5, 30, 33
      Air Squadron 5
      Headquarters Signals 5
    No 1 (RM) Commando 27
    No 40 (RM) Commando 5, 27
    No 41 (RM) Commando 5, 27, 33
    No 42 (RM) Commando 5, 28
    No 43 (RM) Commando 5, 28
    No 44 (RM) Commando 5, 28
    No 45 (RM) Commando 28
    No 46 (RM) Commando 5, 28, 33
    No 47 (RM) Commando 28
    No 48 (RM) Commando 28
    Royal Marine Division 30
    Royal Marines Engineers Commando 29
    Commando Logistics Regiments 5
  Royal Marines Engineers 5
  Royal Marines Labour Corps
    Chatham 43
    Deal 44, 46
  Royal Marine Light Infantry 3
  Royal Marines Medical Unit Personnel 42
  Royal Marine Reserve 3
Royal Marines Section, General Headquarters 2nd Echelon, 21st Army Group 29
Rules and Instructions 4, 5

S

Scheme for Maintaining a Body of Marine-Forces 6
Sea Kit 6
Sheerness Royal Marines' Church, Baptisms 19
Siege Regiment 27
South Africa 19
Special Reports 27
State Papers Domestic, Military Entry Books 38, 42
Statistics 5, 37
Suakin 20
Suez 20
Summaries of Events 26

T

Task Forces, Naval Carrier 32
Toast, Loyal 34
Treasury 1, 6, 22, 23, 40, 52

U

Uniform 6, 7, 36, 52
United Nations Forces 29, 30

W

Walmer 3
War Diaries 26-29
War Establishment, Royal Marine 30, 33
    Hong Kong 30,33
Warrants, Royal 37
Weekly Reports 27